New Life
for an Old House

Other books by Trudy West:

The Young Charles Lamb
The Young Wordsworth
The Timber-framed House in England
The Fireplace in the Home

With love on Your Birthday
Juliet x Camilla xx
Jonathan   David

New Life
for an Old House

Trudy West

Illustrated by Percy W. Blandford

Barrie & Jenkins
London Melbourne Sydney Auckland Johannesburg

Barrie & Jenkins Ltd

An imprint of the Hutchinson Publishing Group

17–21 Conway Street, London W1P 6JD

Hutchinson Group (Australia) Pty Ltd
30–32 Cremorne Street, Richmond South, Victoria 3121
PO Box 151, Broadway, New South Wales 2007

Hutchinson Group (NZ) Ltd
32–34 View Road, PO Box 40–086, Glenfield, Auckland 10

Hutchinson Group (SA) Pty Ltd
PO Box 337, Bergvlei 2012, South Africa

First published 1984
© Trudy West 1984

Set in Monophoto Sabon by Servis Filmsetting Ltd, Manchester

Printed and bound in Great Britain by Anchor Brendon Ltd, Tiptree, Essex

British Library Cataloguing in Publication Data
West, Trudy
    New life for an old house.
    1 Dwellings–Remodelling
    I. Title
    728.3′028′8   TH4816

ISBN 0 09 154130 1

Contents

List of illustrations

FIGURES

Acknowledgements

I am grateful for leave to quote from 'Little Gidding' by T. S. Eliot, by permission of the publishers Faber & Faber.

I should also like to thank the many professional bodies and commercial organizations who assisted me in my research, especially S. J. Boulton & Sons Ltd, Nightingale Homes Ltd, D. C. H. Jones Building Services and Debenham Tewson & Chinnocks.

I particularly wish to acknowledge with gratitude the kindness and courtesy of all those people who allowed me to inspect their homes and to have them photographed, with a special word of thanks to those architects who were so unfailingly helpful, in particular Mr John Boys of the Boys Jarvis Partnership, Mr Andrew G. Black and Mr A. J. Jedwab.

All photographs and line illustrations, unless otherwise specified, are by Percy W. Blandford. The plans of Drumglas and The Old Smithy are reproduced by permission of the Boys Jarvis Partnership; those of Kilmahew by permission of C. J. Selwood; those of The Old School by permission of Roger Softly; and those of The Pump House by permission of Andrew G. Black.

Introduction

In the past few decades we have witnessed the needless destruction of many fine old buildings, victims of the commercial developers, who have offered nothing comparable in place of them. Now, hopefully, the tide has turned, as many more people are active in their efforts to restore old houses and to appreciate their worth. It is to this growing body of restorers that I direct this book, and for them I have included as much practical and useful information as possible.

I have seen all the examples of buildings cited and spoken with the specialized craftsmen whose views and techniques are expressed in the book. I have tried to stress the ideal and uphold the principles of true restoration, and if some of the examples I have chosen seem not to attain these heights, they still reach their objective of giving a renewed lease of life to an old house.

To this end, I have seen as many different types of houses in as many different localities as possible – in England, Scotland and Wales – in order to get a broad view of the subject of restoration in all its aspects, including keeping alive the old crafts.

So, to sum up, in the words of T. S. Eliot:

We shall not cease from exploration
And the end of all our exploring
Will be to arrive where we started
And know the place for the first time.

Perhaps that is the essence of restoration – to look at an old building, know it for the first time, study its origins and its history and to feel an affinity with the past.

I

A General Survey

'If one has a very bitter enemy the best way to revenge oneself is to give him an old house,' runs an old Spanish proverb. It depends, of course, on the old house, but nowadays few people would think it a gift to be despised.

There is, indeed, an increasing trend towards the restoration of old property and a good deal of feeling against its needless destruction. Never before has there been such an interest in old buildings or a desire to know more about them and the essential crafts that went into their making, as more people generally are becoming aware of the truth that we have something intrinsically good, something irreplaceable in our national building heritage which should be preserved before it is too late. We have watched with horrified disbelief the disintegration of the much-vaunted tower blocks that lasted a mere fifteen years, and turned back with relief to the solid reality of period houses – Tudor, Georgian, Victorian, Edwardian – realizing their potential for making the kind of good family homes that are not turned out of a mould.

As a nation we are richly endowed with fine houses of every period. In few other countries can we meet with so many examples of the art of building at its best and most beautiful, and it is a tribute to the quality of the buildings themselves that we have in general cherished them and found ways and means of keeping them intact, despite the constant threat of the bulldozers.

In the past, when transport was both difficult and expensive, local materials were used for building and a vernacular style of architecture grew up which looked exactly right for its setting. It captured the *genius loci* and gave the houses certain distinctive characteristics according to the districts in which they were built. Even their styles were different, speaking an architectural dialect of their own, equal in their way to the native tongue.

In the stone country rubble and ashlar, of sound quality, were put together by masons skilled in their craft. If brick was the local material it was well burnt and laid in excellent mortar. Roof tiles, whether of stone or clay, were made to last. Timber-framed houses were of stout English oak, firmly jointed together by craftsmen and capable of being expanded or modified in plan without weakening their strength. All were built of natural materials which mature and become more beautiful with age, making reconditioning eminently worthwhile.

For this reason restoring an old house can be both stimulating and rewarding, resulting in a house that is unique, a home virtually re-created from the past yet fitting into the present, with the addition of modern conveniences and comforts as an added bonus.

Philip Webb, the eminent nineteenth-century architect, after the restoration of Forthampton Court, Gloucestershire, wrote to the owner, '. . . I think you should rejoice in your fine old house. No new house, even if built by a much finer architect than the one you accidentally employed, could give you half the satisfaction that the old one must. . . .'

That seems to sum it up in a few words – the sense of satisfaction and pride in preserving something that is good, whether it be a cottage or a castle. Still more satisfying is doing most of the work oneself, watching one's dreams become realities as the project takes shape.

This is not just an altruistic sentiment, neither is it meant to be sentimentalism, investing every tumbledown cottage covered with mouldering thatch with an aura of romanticism. Far from it. It does mean that we should have enough insight to penetrate the clutter of the years and see the possibilities ahead, whilst visualizing the kind of home that could emerge from a neglected building after skilful and sympathetic restoration.

On a practical level, it is an obvious economy from all standpoints to make use of good buildings which have many years of service still before them. They are cheaper to buy in the first place and may well qualify for a grant towards the cost of improvement and modernization, which is discussed in later chapters. This way, too, a family is more likely to get the accommodation suited to its personal tastes and needs. In this context it has become accepted practice for people to restore almost any old building which has potential advantages, such as a coach house, barn, stables, windmill, and so on. There is even a restored lime kiln on the coast of Anglesey. All of these make delightful family homes with spacious rooms and ample storage space, as opposed to the often cramped conditions of the average modern house, and they are unique.

Nevertheless, whatever the choice of old building, or however appealing its outward appearance, the intending restorer should not be entirely blind to the practical problems involved. There are certain hard facts to be considered before becoming irrevocably committed to full-scale restoration.

Basically, the most searching question is, is the structure sound? Will it warrant endless time, energy and money being spent on it? Unless you are an expert yourself, the answer lies in a thorough and painstaking survey of the structure by an architect, or at least a competent surveyor, who will assess the state and value of the building. It is essential to know if it has any serious defects and what maintenance costs may be incurred for the future.

Ideally, there should be a study of the building's period and its plan in order to grasp the proper proportions and relationships between its parts. Where a house is very old, or maybe a listed building, a local history society is usually pleased to help with any research, particularly where the building represents the vernacular architecture of a county. Some interesting facts often come to light in this way.

Too often the simple direct planning of an original building has been confused by the thoughtless alterations of a later owner, either through lack of appreciation of its structural meaning or a blindness to its possibilities. Whatever the reason for the confusions, tracing the intentions of the old-time builder will make the preliminary work much more interesting.

An old house of any period will almost certainly contain some original craftsmanship – a wood carving, maybe, some ornamental plasterwork, stonework or metalwork – all of which may need repair or, in some cases, complete replacement. We speak rather too glibly about such features being irreplaceable; they are in the sense that the original is lost for ever, but we should remember that there are many fine modern craftsmen available today who are supremely capable of copying old work, either by building up from a fragment of the original or by working from a photograph or drawing. In this context old pictures and plans are invaluable guides and it is worthwhile inquiring if any are available.

Work of this nature requires highly specialized techniques, matching the new material with the original so that it merges into the general composition of the whole scheme. There is a loss of individuality where mass-produced materials are used. Inferior workmanship, too, can ruin an old theme and destroy the architectural and historical value of a house, but none of this need frighten off anyone who is thinking of restoring an old house which contains architectural treasures, for craftsmen are far from being the dying race that some people would have us believe.

The Crafts Council and the Council for Small Industries in Rural Areas (CoSIRA) are but two of the organizations which exist to put people in touch with local craftsmen who are capable of undertaking restoration work. For the convenience of the reader a list of these and other useful organizations with their addresses is appended at the end of this book.

Of course, the idea of restoring to the 'original' cannot be interpreted too literally. The famous Scottish architect, Robert Weir Schultz, in a letter to *Country Life* in 1905 referring to the proposed restoration of a sixteenth-century yeoman's house in Kent said, 'It would be absurd to attempt to restore it, either outside or in, to its "original" state. To be consistent, one ought to go back to the mud floor, the open fire in the centre of the Hall, the unglazed windows, etc. The 17th century floors, beams, and brick chimneys are part of the history of the place and therefore should be left to tell their tale.' In other words, one must use discretion and commonsense.

The fact that some old houses, particularly cottages, are not conditioned or equipped for modern living is obvious at first sight, and much work may need to be done before they can be made habitable by our present-day standards. The following is a brief summary of the main points to be checked when assessing a house of any period before purchase.

Foundations The condition of the foundations may be judged by the appearance of the walling, where cracks or bulges may betray uneven settlements. It can usually be established if any structural movements are alive or expended by the simple device of sticking 'tell-tales' over them; that is, slips of gummed paper with the date noted on them. They will tear apart in a few days if there is any movement in the walls. Where there is any doubt at all an architect should be consulted about the advisability of underpinning.

Roofs The roof has always been the single most important feature of any house, both as protection and for appearance, and its role does not change. If the roof is ignored, it is at the peril of the structure beneath. The traditional roofing materials will be discussed in more detail in Chapter 5, but in making a preliminary survey the house owner should look for the flaws that tell him that his roof will either need repair or replacement in the near future. He should examine it carefully, outside as well as in, and not be misled by the apparent slightness of the faults he sees. A couple of dislodged slates or tiles may appear trivial but they could indicate more widespread damage.

A few nails that have rusted or slates that have begun to disintegrate may be harbingers of worse to come. After all, the rest of the roof is as old as the original fixings.

Simply to look up at the roof from the garden is not enough. The evidence is often to be found inside – in the roof space or loft, an area of the house once rarely visited, but nowadays put to more use than ever before. The thin shaft of sunlight slipping through the tiles is evidence of movement. More obvious indications of failure are tiny tile or slate fragments on the joists. They are the result of 'spalling' or delamination: water has penetrated the laminar, or layered structure, and frost has begun the process of fragmentation. One decaying tile shifts and exposes another, spreading the 'disease' through the roof.

For all that, old roofs were usually of excellent construction and a few leaks should not condemn a house. It is possible that the covering has suffered from the wear and tear of the years and has probably been patched time and time again, which is no lasting remedy. It may prove cheaper in the long run to renew a roof rather than face the cost of constant repair for leaks, but obviously this is a case for individual assessment.

Fig. 1 *Bulging brick wall, due to the outward thrust of a cross beam. The tie rod is faulty*

Walls The main function of walls, whatever their form, is to keep out the wind and the rain, and therefore they should be examined carefully for cracks in the pointing or other defects. Wind will force the rain through pores and cracks that it might not penetrate normally, so if the house is in an area that is subject to high winds this is a point to note.

In general, the walls of old buildings are more proof against rain and dampness than new ones. Where they are built of stone or brick they are thicker than in modern construction and over the years have acquired a weathered external surface that resists dampness in the atmosphere. The joints must be inspected, however, to make sure they are secure and tight. Note especially where ivy roots or overgrown creepers are destroying a wall.

Floors Floors in old houses, especially timber-framed houses, often have a decided slope in one direction where the house has settled on its earth foundations. Wide boards of oak or elm on joists were used; in late medieval days these were often 18 inches wide and even in Georgian days were still 1 foot or more in width. Such old floorboards are still a beautiful feature of many an old house or cottage. A superficially neglected condition, caused by wear and tear, should not be counted against them. This is a fault that can easily be remedied by polishing and they will well repay the effort. It is the more serious defects that should be looked for: a crack between boards and skirting, for instance, is an indication that the floor has dropped, probably through decay, and the bearings are rotting. This needs more extensive investigation.

Woodworm   Look for piles of bore dust and clean exit holes in timbers. This will point to active beetle infestation which will call for drastic treatment.

Rot   Other signs of decay may be evidence of dry rot or wet rot, both of which are caused by damp.

Damp   This is the worst enemy of old buildings. It is the main cause of decay in most materials, weakening their physical endurance, attracting pests in timber and encouraging fungal growths, and therefore all possible sources of trouble should come under close inspection. Defective gutters and rain pipes are one of the root causes of damage from this trouble. Look also for broken roof tiles or leaky thatching, faulty flashing round chimneys or window sills, cracked or broken rainwater pipes (a rainwater head choked with weeds may cause overflowing), imperfect glazing, a faulty damp-proof course (or none at all), and unventilated floors. All sub-floor ventilation should be checked.

The classic signs of rising damp are seen in the flooring, on skirting boards and plaster on and around the bottom of an exterior wall, where they are noticeably wet. A sooty black mould or even mildew may appear. The cause may be a heap of soil which has built up against a wall, obstructing ventilation, or it may be a blocked air brick, deliberately done by a previous owner in an effort to keep more warmth in the house. Cellars may be damp through under-ventilation for this reason.

In some old cottages the ground floor may be at a lower level than the ground outside, which encourages rising damp. This need not be classed as a major defect, as it can be overcome quite well by sinking a wide path round the outside of the building, making sure that it is properly drained by allowing a sufficient slope for the water to run towards the lowest corner to a drain or a soakaway.

Wells   An old house may have a well and it should be established that this is dry and whether it is open or sealed. It is imperative that it should be made quite safe.

Plumbing and electrical installations These should be checked by an expert in his trade. Amateurs can do untold harm in both these areas, even to the point of being dangerous.

Most of these points are dealt with more fully in the ensuing chapters, but it is as well to bear in mind that however bad a house may look at first sight very few things are incurable. With modern technological advances in the field of preservation there is a remedy for virtually everything.

Where the intention is to get a loan on the house from a building society, their own valuer will be sent to inspect the property and submit a written valuation to the society. This is a condition required by the Building Societies Act in respect of any property offered as security for mortgage. This does not preclude the employment of an independent surveyor by the purchaser, and such a surveyor should be a member of one of the professional bodies such as the Royal Institution of Chartered Surveyors, the Royal Institute of British Architects and the Incorporated Society of Valuers and Auctioneers. This is for your own protection.

Occasionally, where there is extensive rot to be dealt with in a house, a building society will specify that treatment is to be carried out by a specialist firm who will provide a written guarantee. If the work has been done by the householder they have the right to send their valuer to inspect it afterwards. Either way, it is fair to both parties.

There is, of course, much that the average handyman can do for himself, and will enjoy doing, but structural alterations must come within the province of an architect, who will draw up plans for his client's approval. Some people say, why use an architect? The short answer is that he is a specialist trained to use his design skills and imagination to translate his client's ideas into practice. His knowledge of planning and building problems can often avoid underestimating or overspending. Finding the right architect for the job – male or female – costs nothing. The Clients' Advisory Service of the Royal Institute of British Architects is always pleased to help.

Even so, there is no reason why the householder should not do the work of which he is capable, if he wants to cut costs, and working under the aegis of an architect in this way can be very rewarding and pleasurable.

Bear in mind always that an old house looks its worst during the preparation period, but this is the time to look ahead and anticipate the day when it will be a home and not a rubbish dump. Making a house warm, weatherproof and sanitary must take priority. The other restoration work can follow as and when time and money permit. In the main, it is best to move into a house as soon as possible, even though it may mean a good deal of discomfort to begin with. Those who have tried it say that only by living in a house for at least six months can you really plan the rooms to the best advantage, to make them as convenient and labour-saving as possible. Basic factors such as light, possible traffic noises, the position of plumbing, windows, doors, cupboards, etc., can then be assessed in the light of experience. It is a grave mistake to make major alterations before having tested all possibilities. The layout of a kitchen, for example, or the position of a new bathroom, should be absolutely definite before new plumbing is installed. It makes all the difference to whoever is running the home.

While discovering the full potentialities of a house in this way you can still leave yourself free to plot the rooms in imagination. There may be some special pieces of furniture to be placed to the best advantage, some treasured ornaments or pictures to be displayed – there are a hundred small things to take into account that add up to making a house into a home.

Some period houses seem to have been designed with more of a regard for symmetry and stateliness than for convenience and comfort. Pope wrote satirically on this subject:

'Tis very fine,
But where d'ye sleep or where d'ye dine?
I find by all you have been telling,
That 'tis a house and not a dwelling.

Now, even this kind of house can be made into a modern home very successfully. No matter whether it is dignified Regency or the not-so-humble cottage, some research at the planning stage will avoid disappointment later on, and in this respect the home-interest magazines can be very helpful with hints and ideas.

In some cases it is necessary to get planning permission from the local authority for any alterations, particularly where listed buildings are concerned (see Chapter 13). Local building regulations should be consulted, together with the law governing some ancient buildings. The law may be different in some respects in Scotland and Wales and it is wise to make quite certain of the rules to be observed before plunging into full-scale restoration. Then, with a definite goal in mind and the necessary preliminaries completed, work can begin without further hindrance.

2
The Timber-framed House

Timber-framed houses, with their delightful profusion of beams, posts and decorations, are usually associated in our minds with the Tudor period, that flamboyant age when wealth was beginning to be more evenly distributed and men expressed their new-found freedom in the carefree way in which they built their houses.

It was in fact in the fifteenth, sixteenth and seventeeth centuries that timber building took on an ease and grace that has never been bettered in any form. The material was plentiful and easy to come by in those areas that were thickly afforested, with the result that timber was used lavishly, with a total disregard for future supplies. Houses of all sizes, from the elaborate manor to the single-bay hall house, were built during the great Tudor building boom, and because of the toughness of the material and the method of construction, many survive to this day.

Seeing an old timber-framed house in its skeleton form is like looking at a jigsaw puzzle. All the parts fit together and interlock one with the other in a flowing pattern that traces its chequered history over the years. Designs were both flexible and adaptable, carrying the weight of the superstructure on their stout posts and capable of being expanded or modified at will to suit a family's current requirements. That is why they are so fascinating to restore, why each one is so intensely individual. They were not the products of architects; they just grew as the owners wanted them, without any perceptible plan. Now, twentieth-century owners are rediscovering them, restoring the centuries-old timbers to their former glory and giving the old houses a new lease of life and a new page in their history.

Broadly speaking, there were two types of timber construction: the jettied style, which was built storey by storey, each one overhanging the last; or that built on the later 'balloon' principle, with no overhang and with wider-spaced studs, or posts, reaching to the eaves, stiffened by diagonal braces and with infillings of wattle and daub or brick nogging between the studs.

Certainly the jetty was the most pleasant fashion, if only because it gave the carpenter unending opportunities to display his skill in the fashioning of a corner post or brackets, the moulding of a fascia board and other individual details. In fact, any timber-framed house in the Middle Ages tended to be decorated and carved wherever it was possible for the craftsman to find a space, for it was an age renowned for its good craftsmanship, much of which has never been surpassed. Each county had its own distinctive style, dictated to a certain extent by the availability of local materials, but even more by the personal methods and preferences of the builder, all of which has left us with a delightful legacy of vernacular architecture.

All the houses were built of stout English oak, with beams, posts and joists mortised and tenoned together, and made secure by wooden pegs of heart of oak firmly driven through holes made by an auger. Not a nail was used anywhere in frame assembly. As a rule the medieval carpenter cut, prepared and put together the timbers of the frame in his own yard, marking the joints ready for assembly on site. The heavy joints were numbered with a system of Roman numerals (Arabic numerals were unknown until the time of the Renaissance), usually made with a tool called a scribe. The system was simple but effective and the craftsmen were able to follow it without difficulty when it came to erecting the timbers and fitting the matching parts of a joint together. In surviving medieval buildings the carpenters' marks are often still visible, particularly in the roof timbers. If they run in sequence it indicates an original structure; if they are not in sequence, it probably points to some rearrangements in the way of alterations or extensions in past times.

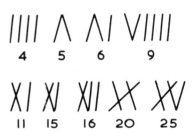

Fig. 2 *Medieval carpenters' marks, cut with a scribe*

Inside the roof space the timber trusses were often elaborate and decorative. Like the frame, they were usually prefabricated, then dismantled and reassembled on site. They were mostly of oak, but chestnut was used occasionally.

This gives a brief idea of the general pattern of building that the owner of a timber-framed house may expect to find, but much evidence of the original structure may be hidden until the work of restoration actually begins. The way in which timbers are fastened together, and the position of the principal posts, main beams and girders should be a guide to the builder's intentions, but other features may often be detected through the unusual thickness of a partition wall. This may conceal a Tudor fireplace, a staircase wall, or hall screens. A wall that sounds hollow when tapped invariably merits investigation, and the stripping down of wallpapers may reveal some painted murals or early panelling, which are likely to be valuable.

Fig. 3 *Medieval carpenters' marks, with circles and segments added with a compass to denote the position of a timber*

Inspecting the timbers It should be remembered that the texture of oak is moderately open and rather uneven, which gives it a tendency to warp. Over the years this causes a certain amount of irregularity and distortion in the appearance of old timbers, but it is this very irregularity which gives old beams their visual appeal. Provided that the joints are safe it is better to accept a somewhat eccentric appearance than to court disaster by unnecessary interference. Timbers should never be forced back into position.

Oak also has a tendency to crack along the grain, which does no harm at all. If the cracks are wide they can be caulked, but *never* with cement. It will not only ruin the appearance of the wood but it will provide a reservoir of damp in wet weather.

There is always a certain amount of movement in a timber-framed building, and this is normal. If, however, it appears to be excessive, it could be due to the pegs which pin the medieval tenons together working loose. This can be cured by knocking the pegs home hard or by replacing them with new, slightly tapered pegs cut oversize for the hole and left projecting a little – not trimmed off flush. If the original pegs have perished they must be drilled out first before being renewed.

Sometimes empty mortises are found on old beams, but this does not necessarily mean a missing member. It may indicate a reused beam, for a great many fine heavy beams were taken out of medieval houses when they were 'modernized' in the late seventeenth century and these second-hand timbers were frequently used by the old builders.

In some cases it may be found that the ground floor of a jettied type of house has been enlarged to match the floors above, and any sign of weakening of the structure as a result of this extension should be corrected, particularly where posts have been removed. In the same way upper floors may be weakened by the removal of gables which help to balance them.

A close inspection of an old roof can lead to the discovery of some lost features, not all of them welcome. For instance, it may reveal that a tie beam has been severed at some time to make a doorway or staircase, and if this is the case the beam should be made good without delay lest the walls bulge and the roof collapse for want of its support. Possibly a chimney stack has been taken away, leaving trimmed openings in the ceilings; traces of soot where the flues were confirm this theory.

Some old houses, particularly those in towns, have suffered greatly from past restorers' efforts to 'modernize' them, without regard to the structure. A succession of plumbers, hot-water engineers, gas fitters and electricians have in turn cut away the fabric to complete their particular job and very often have weakened the whole structure in so doing. For example, gas pipes, water pipes and electric cables have to be laid well clear of the floorboards, and it has sometimes been found that the workman in question has either cut or drilled a passageway for his materials right through a beam vitally necessary for the safety of the building. (Amateur electricians are the worst offenders in this respect.) He has conformed with the regulation to keep clear of the boards but in so doing has endangered the structure in other ways. The removal or mutilating of a brace or strut, or even a whole load-bearing partition, by some past enthusiast may cause sagging or eventual collapse.

These are some examples of the common errors that should be looked for and rectified as soon as possible, for it is essential for the basic structure of the house to be sound or the whole purpose of restoration will be defeated.

Damp   Damp is the most common cause of weakness in structural timbers, and it often brings in its train those twin evils, fungal and beetle attack. Their treatment is dealt with in detail in Chapter 10. There is need for an efficient damp-proof course in any house and in addition every opportunity should be taken to introduce adequate ventilation. In a timber-framed house this is particularly important between timbers such as wall plates and walling which may be damp. New timbers should never be set in contact with damp walling – the cause of the dampness must be eliminated first.

A timber-framed house covered with plaster, hanging tiles or weatherboarding should not be affected by damp unless the outer skin is broken; but exposed framing, without and within, having panels filled with plaster or brick nogging, needs some care to exclude the weather. To cover such framing would be a mistake, but it should be protected from damp. Providing each panel with vertical drainage in the form of a groove in the oak will often suffice and will help to avoid the formation of pools of water on the tops of horizontal timbers.

In earlier types of jettied buildings the projecting floor joists were protected by long horizontal boards known as fascia boards, beautifully moulded, and some of these remain in good condition. When the idea was eventually abandoned, the ends of the joists were left simply rounded off and therefore vulnerable to damp.

Decay   Structural timbers should also be examined carefully for signs of decay. First, look closely at the feet of rafters in the roof, where any trouble will cause the ridge to sag; also look at the joints between the rafters and the ties, and similar vulnerable points. The main sills and the feet of the main posts, where the grain end of timber is susceptible to damp, should receive particular attention and be well protected from weather penetration.

Damage to beams by decay can sometimes be covered by a patch, but it must be done very skilfully, using the same species of timber as the original so that the new wood blends in with the old. There is usually plenty of thickness to old timbers, which allows a certain amount of repair work to be done with safety, but even so, great care should be taken not to overstep the limits. Where beams have to be replaced in their entirety it is best to use salvaged material which will match and be well seasoned for such restoration work. There is usually some sound second-hand oak to be found in the country, in rural builders' yards and elsewhere, which is ideal for the purpose.

One enterprising young couple, restoring a medieval house on a limited budget, found most of their materials on local skips when similar old buildings were being demolished. What one person throws away as useless may well be just the thing the do-it-yourself restorer is looking for, and in most cases it will be good, authentic material, absolutely right for the job. Another advantage in watching a demolition take place is that it provides an excellent opportunity to study the techniques and materials that were used in a past age.

The rural small builder, as a rule, is quite a collector of useful bits and pieces, and is also a mine of information on likely supplies from derelict buildings, so his acquaintance is worth cultivating.

Cleaning Oak used externally will weather best if left alone. It should never be oiled, for after a time it will look stained, the grain will open and it will turn black on the surface.

If oak needs no special preservative treatment externally, it may be a different matter internally where badly neglected old timbers are in need of cleaning. They may be encrusted with a hard deposit of dirt that will need a thorough scraping to remove – a Dutch hoe was used for the purpose by one lady – but where such drastic scraping is unnecessary an ordinary sanding will usually suffice. Once the rough surface has been cleaned down, some architects recommend the application of a coat of linseed oil. One enthusiast was heard to say that she used boot polish on her beams because 'it gives the impression of having been caressed by loving hands over the centuries'. No doubt the boot polish, with its preservative qualities, would do no harm to the timbers, but one quails at the thought of the hours of work involved in such treatment for a house of any size.

Removing paint from old timbers requires time and patience. Continuous wire brushing along the grain followed by sanding will usually remove the last traces of paint, and all that will be required then is a coating of oil and insecticide, depending upon their condition.

Cladding   The standard medieval method of cladding was by filling in the spaces between the timber studs with panels of wattle and daub. It was so satisfactory that the rural builders stuck to it long after more sophisticated ways had been introduced, and many an old timber-framed house today has its original wattle and daub walls intact, preserved under successive coats of plaster and acting as a perfect insulator.

The wattle consisted of a screen of interlaced willow or hazel rods, but the composition of the daub varied. Some of the earliest forms were simply made of mud and cow dung, which contained a certain amount of straw, but tow or hair from virtually any animal was used equally well as a binding agent. The daub was applied in layers, pressed well into the crevices of the wattling. It was apt to shrink and crack after it dried, so a thin coat of lime plaster mixed with cow hair was applied to seal the cracks and give it a better finish. Probably a coat of whitewash was added for good measure, for the medieval builder loved whitewash.

Obviously it is impossible to restore wattle and daub to its original form, but where it is found in good condition it can safely be left and given an additional coat of plaster to strengthen it. It is more usual these days to replace damaged panels with plasterboard, with a layer of some insulation material behind it, placed between the studs, then to give it a further skim coat.

The ideal was to use nothing but lime plaster for all restoration work, following the style of the old builders, but this is no longer possible because of the high cost involved, and nearly all architects have now come to regard plasterboard as an acceptable alternative. It is simply a sandwich of gypsum plaster between two sheets of paper, its only drawback being that it is a poor insulator against noise. But its cost is reasonable and it is easy to use.

It may in fact be desirable to plaster the wall timbers within a room in order to keep out draughts, especially if the walls are of the kind that were originally clothed – probably for a good reason – and some overenthusiastic past restorer has exposed them again. In this case, when replastering is done it should be applied to split laths – sawn laths might snap under the stress of movement usually present in timber-framed buildings.

In some areas building regulations forbid the use of exposed timbering on both sides, because of fire risks. It is a point to be checked. In such cases the restorer must choose between one or the other.

When existing plastering is showing signs of disintegrating it should be stripped down completely and renewed; but where repair work is all that is necessary the composition of the original plaster should be noted and copied as far as possible, to avoid obvious and unsightly patches. In this case it may be advisable to consult an expert rather than spoil the job.

With these general principles in mind the restoration of an old timber-framed house can best be illustrated by some actual examples. One at Great Bardfield, Essex, is a case in point.

The house, now called by its original name, Gobions, was built around 1551. It is a benign-looking building, long and narrow, with close-set timbers of silvery weathered oak and plastered panels inset between them, facing the village High Street. Its mellow tiled roof has a central chimney stack with four grouped diagonal shafts, put in about a century after the house was built.

Like so many similar houses it has changed its appearance more than once in the course of the years, to suit the whims of the owners, who were no doubt anxious to keep up with the styles of the day. It had been plastered over in Georgian times, hung with brick and tile and given sash windows in Edwardian days, before being returned to its original timbered appearance in the 1930s, but with diamond-paned lattice windows instead of the old mullions. Although the mullions were a loss, aesthetically speaking, the lattices were a distinct improvement in that they allowed more light and air into the rooms while being still sympathetic to the architecture. The reinstatement of a Tudor oak front door completed the exterior.

The interior, however, was a mixture of Georgian and Victorian styles, with all the old beams, except one, covered in. The present owners, visualizing what it could be like, decided to put the rooms back into character, at the same time bringing the house up to date in essential conveniences.

The owner took a year off from his business and with the help of his wife and one handyman did all the work himself, indulging his love of carpentry as he restored the splendid old woodwork to its prime.

As with all medieval houses of this type it had been built straight on to the earth, with no damp-proof course, and the oak floorboards in the sitting room were rotten. To counteract this, a concrete raft was inserted under the house as far as possible and a trench dug all round the outside to provide extra drainage and ventilation in the form of air bricks. The floor was relaid with pine boards and eventually the room was close-carpeted.

Although the rooms were large they looked dull and featureless, dominated by heavy, black marble fireplaces that looked out of place, and wallpapers that were not right for their setting. The fireplaces were taken out, not without some difficulty; although great care was taken they were broken in the final stages of being pulled out. Behind them, as had been hoped, were the huge open brick fireplaces so typical of the Tudors, and these were restored to the original state, with their small Tudor bricks cleaned and repointed.

1 *Gobions, Great Bardfield, Essex, restored to its original half-timbered appearance*

The wallpapers were stripped down and the underlying plaster chipped off to expose the old beams and studs, some with carpenters' marks and the marks of the adze still seen clearly on them, and all secured by wooden pegs. They were all surprisingly sound and no more than one or two structural timbers had to be renewed, using good, seasoned, old wood.

Some of the timbers showed signs of woodworm and this was quickly dealt with by means of the appropriate preservative treatment. Where the wood was too badly affected to be left, it was cut out, burnt, and replaced by a patch that exactly matched the original wood.

Some of the original wattle and daub panels were still in good condition, sound enough to leave where the old-time craftsmen had put them over three hundred years ago. With an additional coat of plaster they were well protected for who knows how many more years to come. For all that, most of the old plastering had to be replaced by new, and this was done by inserting a layer of insulation behind a plasterboard panel, which was given a skim coat and placed between the timbers.

Over the years beams in every part of the house had accumulated a thick crust of dirt and the method of cleaning in this case was to scrape them with a plumber's shave hook which did not damage the wood. Where extra cleaning was needed, nothing but water was used.

One of the dirtiest jobs was cleaning inside the roof, where the timbers were coated with a quarter of an inch of soot – proof, if any were needed, of the existence of a central fire in the hall below. When all the soot and rubble were cleared away the full beauty of the medieval construction could be appreciated, which included two original trusses with chamfered tie beams, king posts with moulded capitals and bases, and four-way struts (Plate 2). After cleaning, all the timbers, in common with those in the rest of the house, were sprayed with preservative which effectively killed off all pests, including some deathwatch beetle. The roof covering was still sound and watertight, and it was interesting to see that the old clay tiles had been bedded on hay, some wisps of which were hanging down, still in good condition. This was an old method of bedding tiles which was obviously very effective, for it looked as if it would be a long time before this particular roof would need replacement.

The original building had a hall open to the roof, with a central chimney stack inserted probably in the late sixteenth century. During one of the early renovations there had been a partition wall put up in a bedroom to make an extra room, and it was when this dividing wall

2 *One of the fine original king posts in the roof of Gobions. Tiles were bedded down on hay, some wisps of which can still be seen*

was removed that an exciting discovery was made in the form of two beautifully carved medieval bosses on the inner end of each one of the original 'hammer' beams which had been hidden when the upper floor was put in. The carvings are of heads, one male and one female, the features and head-dresses still perfectly detailed: the woman wears the square, crimped coif of that period. They may be portraits of the original owners, but they are too beautiful to remain hidden under a floor, so the floorboards were cut away to make a lighted recess at each end. Now they can be seen at will.

At the other end of the room a further unusual feature was uncovered when the plaster was stripped off the inner face of the external wall. It was a saltire, or bracing, in the form of a St Andrew's Cross, the timbers very wide and sturdy and in excellent condition. These, too, were left exposed, and the walls replastered in between

3 The division between two rooms in Gobions was removed from the 'hammer beam' frame to make one large bedroom. These beams have carved bosses on their inner ends, concealed when the floor was put in

them. This bedroom, opened up to its original size, was now large enough to take a partition wall down one side of it to accommodate two new bathrooms, one *en suite* with the principal bedroom, and the other, with access from the landing, for the convenience of guests.

The guest room also yielded its discoveries when an unusual beam was uncovered on one wall. On it was a painted inscription in meticulous Elizabethan lettering in white across the whole length of a 17-foot beam. Scrupulous care was taken in its cleaning, inch by inch, but even so, it is not possible to decipher the lettering with any degree of accuracy. Is it perhaps one of the moral exhortations of which the Elizabethans were so fond? Or is it a memorial, or simply some instructions to the guest, warning him how to behave, after the style of Thomas Tusser, the Elizabethan versifier? We shall never know, but it makes a good talking point for guests.

Downstairs, on the ground floor, a dividing partition was removed in the sitting room to make one large room facing south-east and north-west, so that it gets all the available sunshine. The removal of this wall meant that the ceiling had to be reinforced with an extra beam and post, for safety's sake. It was a major job to erect this beam for it had to be of sound old oak, tremendously thick and heavy, to take the load. All one day was spent in marking out the timber, making sure meanwhile that the ceiling was well supported. Then the new beam was raised on an adjustable jack and plasterer's boards and securely bolted into the wall, with the post adjusted to give additional support. This opens up the room in the best possible way, without detracting from its character.

Originally the front door also opened into this sitting room, with a very small entry space, but this had previously been sealed up and a porch built on at the rear to serve as a main entrance. Since there is a road at the side of the house it was a much more sensible idea and more in keeping with a country house of this size. There was also an unwanted door at the top end of the sitting room, beside the new entrance, and this too was sealed up to make the back wall of a clothes cupboard in the hall – a very useful addition. Another innovation was to make a bar with two-way doors in the wall between the sitting room and the dining room. It is so well concealed in the old panelling that no one would guess it is there until it is opened to dispense hospitality.

The dining room, in the oldest part of the house, is distinguished by a magnificent moulded ceiling beam, dated about 1500, which was reset at some time. It is carved with a twisted leaf design that has been brought out to perfection in the course of restoration. The other notable feature is the great 'hole in the wall' Tudor fireplace which was revealed after the black marble chimneypiece was taken out. It looks so right for its setting that one hopes it will never again be covered in.

All doors throughout the house were stripped down to their original pine and given a satin-finished woodseal. The staircase, of a later date, was given the same treatment. What makes the whole house so attractive, so welcoming, is the furnishing, a discreet mixture of old and new which blends comfort with beauty. The owners have gone to enormous trouble to choose pieces that are just right for a period house of this type.

It was not possible, or even desirable, to restore the old kitchen quarters, so these have been completely refurbished and brought right up to date, with all the latest equipment installed. A useful meals corner, in pine, now stands in the recess once occupied by a large Aga range. Beyond this is a large food and fruit store, half below ground level, and reached by an easy-going flight of stairs. It is an ingenious use of the old solid-fuel store and a boon in a country house where large stocks need to be kept in hand. Modernization also included rewiring, replumbing and the installation of oil-fired central heating.

Outside, at the side of the house, a terrace has been formed with wide, curved steps in York stone leading to the garden and an open loggia, made from the old thatched stables.

This brief description of a lovely country house that has emerged from a medieval building proves that it pays to look beyond outward appearances.

Another type of timber frame was weatherboarded, or clapboarded, a method which was sometimes used when further weatherproofing was needed for the walls. The horizontal boarding overlapped to protect the frame from driving rain. These houses are generally quite small, probably once used as cottages for workers.

The studs of the softwood frame are placed fairly close together in order to take the external boarding and the interior skin of lath and plaster. They are strengthened at the angles by braces, and joints are simply halved, lapped and nailed. It was a cheap and economical way of building in timber and large numbers of these houses appeared in the south-east of England about the time of the Regency.

I found an excellent example in Court Lees Cottage, Staple Cross, East Sussex. Built in the early eighteenth century, it is typical of its kind – a compact, square cottage with white-painted weatherboarding and an old peg tiled roof, standing in an attractive garden, but formerly in need of extensive restoration.

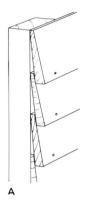

A

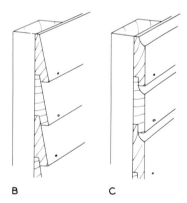

B   C

Fig. 4 A. *Plain weatherboarding, tapered and overlapped* B. *Clapboarding: rabbeted weatherboarding, which allows the boards to fix flat* C. *Shiplap: modern planed parallel rabbeted weatherboarding*

4 *Court Lees Cottage, Staple Cross, East Sussex, with the new kitchen extension. The original weatherboarding consists of long, unbroken planks, with no joins anywhere*

Originally the cottage consisted of two small rooms on the ground floor with the entrance leading directly into the sitting room. The kitchen was a tiny cupboard-like place beside the dining room and a staircase was literally 'cased' in behind a cupboard at the back. Steep stairs – a typical feature of the period – led up to the bedrooms. Everywhere the beams were plastered over and covered with wallpaper – even on the ceilings. It was all hideously out of keeping, the patterned papers creating a claustrophobic effect in a small space. Nevertheless, the new owners lived in it as it was, while making up their minds what they wanted done.

First, they consulted an architect who drew up plans for the constructional work, which was approved by the local authority.

The cottage was obviously damp and the previous owner had built a concrete path all round it which did nothing to cure it. A trench was dug to investigate and this revealed that the cottage had no good foundations – the weatherboarding was virtually sitting on clay soil. The local builder dug down deeply, jacked the cottage up on stilts and stripped the bottom rows of boards off, together with the interior plaster. This was all to the good, for a patch of wet rot was found in one corner and the timbers there had to be cut out drastically and burnt. It was a simple matter to put down a concrete damp-proof course and build up a few courses of bricks at earth level. New oak was slotted into the footings and bottoms of studs before the props were taken out, allowing the building to settle back on to its new foundations. It is now very solid and damp-proof.

At the same time, an extension for a new kitchen was built at the side of the house by knocking through a cupboard beside the fireplace. It was weatherboarded to match the original exactly, so that it merges in as if it had always been there. A stable door in place of the nondescript existing one and a boarded porch completed the exterior which, painted in white, looks very trim.

For the interior, the two small rooms were made into one by removing the partition wall. The supporting beam above the wall was strengthened with an additional iron girder. The beam was in bad condition and it would have been risky to take it down, so it was all concealed in a wood casing and propped up on each side with railway sleepers. Sanded, stained and polished, it is difficult to detect their original use, and they are enormously strong. This has successfully opened up these rooms and made one very light and pleasant living room. Another great improvement was made here by removing an inefficient room heater and opening up the original wide inglenook fireplace to take a blazing log fire, a process which is described more fully in Chapter 6.

Stripping off several layers of wallpapers and hacking off plaster to expose the old beams was a major job and required much patience. All the timbers had been limewashed and the lime had to be scraped off, using a scraper and a wire brush; then they were sanded with an electric sander, given a coating of Cuprinol to guard against woodworm, and finally stained with a Jacobean dark oak stain. Now they look as they must have looked two hundred years ago, in a natural, simple setting.

One or two minor shocks awaited the owners, like, for instance, finding a beam that was resting only on a window. This had to be propped up on a steel girder and is now concealed under new plaster.

Fig. 5 *The new foundations of Court Lees Cottage, Staple Cross*

The original lath and plaster construction was neither soundproof nor warm, so a thick layer of glass-fibre insulating material was placed in each panel between timbers, including ceilings, then covered with a plasterboard panel which was given a skim coat of plaster, and finally painted white. This has made the cottage very cosy and much more soundproof.

Most of the windows and the boarded doors are original. Some had to be repaired by the local joiner, who copied the regional style, and all the old latches and hinges were taken off, cleaned and retained as they were. Where new ones were necessary, as on the front door, they were specially made by the local blacksmith, to match the original.

The old cottage cupboard staircase remains as it was. It would have destroyed the period atmosphere if it had been opened up, as so many people suggested. Upstairs, the bedrooms have been given the same treatment as the living room, with the exception of the third small room, which has been converted into a modern bathroom. The room downstairs that served as a bathroom for the previous owners now forms part of the new kitchen, and the old kitchen is a guest bedroom. It is all a very clever use of space, to get the best possible results.

In the beginning, all drains were tested and put to rights, and as work proceeded the necessary rewiring was done, with the wires concealed and new plumbing put in. In the new kitchen, fully equipped with up-to-date units, is a splendid wood-burning stove which cooks and supplies endless hot water for all domestic purposes as well as radiators in all main rooms.

All this work has gone on over a period of time, in well-planned stages, to suit the convenience of the owners, who did most of the work themselves, with help when needed from the local builder and joiner. In no other way could they have got the kind of cottage they wanted at the price they were prepared to pay. All in all, Court Lees Cottage is an excellent and faithful restoration, well planned and well executed.

One cannot be too didactic about dating old cottages. Some of them, particularly in the south-east, appear to belong to the eighteenth century when they are in fact much older. This is because the Georgians' enthusiasm for the regular classical style led them to alter their cottages and houses to look 'modern' and they used weatherboarding, tiles or sometimes whole façades of brick to cover the original timber framing. There is a delightful example of this 'changing its mind' attitude in an old house called Long Candovers, in the hamlet of Hartley Mauditt, Hampshire. Records go back to 1369, although there is little or nothing left of that period now, except some interesting local history.

The house, which was originally three cottages made into one, has been much altered over the centuries and is now a marvellous medley of styles. Basically, it is timber-framed, with some brick and random stone walls added at different times, with one wall entirely hung with tiles, presumably to weatherproof it at some stage. The crevices behind these tiles are the homes of a great number of small bats which fly out at night on their regular foraging expeditions. The owners counted up to 187 one warm summer's evening, but they leave them undisturbed, knowing that bats are the natural enemy of the deathwatch beetle and their presence means their timbers are protected from this pest. The mellow old tiled roof is half hipped, with a long, sweeping 'catslide' (lean-to) at one side to add to its irregular charm.

The interior is surprisingly roomy, with unexpected little steps leading to unexpected rooms, in one of which no less than three sets of floorboards were discovered, laid one upon another. All had to be treated for woodworm and some new windows were put in, but they are faithful copies of the old, made by a local joiner.

In the sitting room is a vast inglenook, with a bread oven 4 feet deep at one side and a salt box at the other side. The space is now occupied by a huge wood-burning stove which never goes out in winter.

Essential modernization has been done so discreetly that it merges in with the old building as if it had always been there, which is the ultimate test of success. Altogether this is a charming house, difficult to pinpoint, difficult to assess architecturally, but one rejoices that it has fallen into the hands of such discerning and sympathetic owners, which, after all, is what restoration is all about.

Another example of this tendency to camouflage a timber-framed house is seen again in Great Bardfield, Essex. Town House, as it is called, dates from the early seventeenth century: the date 1609 is inscribed on a gable. It was originally the town hall where the 'Borough' courts were held, hence the name. It is now listed as being of architectural or historical interest, warranting a mention in the Royal Commission of Historical Monuments, and thus is protected by law. The plan is L-shaped with the wings extending towards the south-west and north-west. The south-west wing is of a slightly later date and it is probable that it was altered in the eighteenth century, when it was given the beautifully symmetrical principal elevation facing the street, reminiscent of the Georgian period of architecture (Plate 5). Nevertheless, the construction is a heavy timber frame clothed with lath and plaster. As in all houses of this kind, the timbers are difficult to detect until one notices a thickening at the tops of the tall corner posts and a slight projection at roof level.

The house has had a succession of restorers over the years, some obviously misguided ones, but many original features remain, such as a battened door of oak, a fragment of linen-fold panelling and some interesting bosses, beautifully carved. A great many cupboards were found, some quite cavernous and built deeply into the thick walls. A few also had smaller cupboards within them, which raised an interesting query as to their past use.

Apart from the routine treatment of all the timbers, overhauling the wiring and some new plumbing where necessary, restoration has consisted of bringing the original features back to good condition.

5   *Town House, Great Bardfield, Essex, has a typical Georgian facade over the original old timber frame*

KEN LONG F.S.A.I

TOWN HOUSE GREAT BARDFIELD

Many of the doors and some of the panelling on the upstairs landing had been painted with a dark-colour paint. This was stripped off very carefully and taken back to the original pine, leaving the old regional-style latches and hinges intact. Some unsuitable papers were stripped from the bedroom walls, which were then replastered and painted with magnolia emulsion paint, making them considerably lighter. Leading off the corridor landing is an unusual staircase which branches into two parts a little more than half-way down, one part leading to the kitchen quarters, the other to the back of the entrance hall, where it is concealed behind a door. The owners resisted all suggestions to have this staircase resited, preferring to keep it as it was, an obvious addition to conform to the original hall house frame.

The greatest change has come about in the kitchens, where it was possible to make a comfortable breakfast room from the old kitchen and a new kitchen from the scullery or dairy. Originally these rooms had back-to-back open fireplaces with an axial chimney stack. Now a closed stove has been installed in the opening in the breakfast room, and an oil-fired boiler for the central heating in the aperture in the kitchen, an arrangement that works very well. The original larder, at the foot of the stairs, was so large that it has been made into a very comfortable second bathroom, and in addition there are still many capacious store cupboards, wine stores and the like, of a kind that would never be possible in a modern house.

Thus the idea that restoration of a medieval building will result only in discomfort has been completely exploded by these and many other excellent examples that can be seen around the countryside. Their delight is in their total lack of uniformity and their usefulness in their capacity to be adapted to suit current needs without losing their identity. That is why so many traditional timber-framed houses are being rescued and used as homes once again.

3
The Brick-built House

An old brick building is a decoration in itself. Usually it has mellowed and improved with the years, taking on a weathered, irregular look that is very pleasing to the eye, giving it a 'comfortable' appearance. Its bricks are a variety of soft, warm shades, each one individually made, the work of a craftsman, for until about 130 years ago every brick was made entirely by hand in a local setting.

At one time it was common practice for brickmakers to travel round the country making bricks as they were required. They tested the local clay, blended it and treated it where necessary, and generally adapted their techniques to suit their material. Gradually a great number of small brickyards came into existence and many of the larger country estates had their own brickworks where they made the bricks and brick tiles as they were needed, usually in a field near the building site. But the history of hand-made bricks goes back much farther – as far as the castles, villas and public buildings of the Romans. The art died out with their departure and did not return to any great extent until the fifteenth century, when the first great age of English brickwork began. At that time many an old timber-framed building was given a new façade of brick, and brick nogging began to replace wattle and daub as infilling between timbers – and very decorative it looked, too. The bricks would be laid in patterns – herringbone, chevron or vertical – to follow the new fashion, but these early bricks were a good deal thinner than they are now. In 1477 it was declared by statute that the measurements of a burnt brick should be $8\frac{1}{2} \times 4 \times 2\frac{1}{2}$ inches – the most convenient size and shape for a man to grasp with one hand. They were not very regular in size or shape and were quite roughly finished, so that they had a distinctive rugged texture. They were also a warm orangey-red colour, which came partly from being burnt with wood fuel in a kiln.

The tax on bricks imposed by George III in 1784 caused bricks to be made much larger; since all sizes incurred the same tax the people did all they could to avoid paying more than they needed. The situation changed again in 1803 when double the tax was required for larger bricks. After this, the size settled down to 9 × 4½ × 3 inches, which is slightly larger than modern ones, but was still reckoned to be a convenient size to handle. This is borne out by the slight creases one sees in an old brick which suggest that it had been held in the craftsman's hand while still pliable. Late Victorian bricks are identifiable by the shallow 'frog' – that is, an indentation on one surface to make it easier to position in laying. There are much more pronounced frogs on modern bricks.

Any of the bricks mentioned may be found in an old house. It would be difficult to date a building from this evidence alone, for there may be some bricks of all ages in a single house, possibly due to rebuilding efforts on the part of previous restorers. For all that, a good deal of fine brickwork of the fifteenth and sixteenth centuries survives, and the householder who possesses it should make sure it is preserved, particularly if it is the decorative carved and moulded work so beloved of the Tudors. At that time they used bricks in various shapes for elaborately ornamented chimney stacks, corners, fireplaces, window jambs and other architectural features. They moulded the clay in wooden moulds which were often quite complicated in design. If it was not worth making a special mould, the bricks were shaped with a brick axe, called a scutch, and this was used for the fine decorative bricks which had to be carved. To do this they built large rectangular blocks – softer and finer in texture than ordinary walling bricks – into the wall to form projections, which were then carved back to the desired pattern.

Tudor chimney stacks were especially beautiful and it is good to note that there are a great many left on quite ordinary houses today, particularly in the south-east of England. The bricklayer, a new craftsman in those far-off days, was eager to exercise his skill and he made his chimneys appealing to the eye as well as practical. He introduced endless ways of moulding and shaping the clay before firing it to the form desired, and so produced some of the most beautiful and distinctive chimneys of any age. There was quite a craze for fancy shapes and forms – octagonal, square, circular, fluted or spiral – the surfaces enriched with a variety of raised designs, anything from chevrons, zigzags and diamonds to Tudor roses and heraldic badges. The chimney stacks of the Tudor kitchens at Hampton Court Palace are a fine example of their kind. Although scarcely one is original they are such faithful copies of the fantastic designs of the sixteenth-century bricklayer that they may be said to represent his work, and certainly they are a tribute to the skill of the present-day craftsmen who restore them.

Fig. 6   *Hand-made decorative moulded bricks for building into patterns*

This more elaborate moulded work in all its forms was later copied with Renaissance details, much used at the time of Wren. Many of these details were again copied on Victorian buildings and there was a short-lived revival in the early twentieth century, which means that we may come across ornamental brickwork, ranging from simple patterning to the most intricate carving, on almost any brick building up to the Edwardian period.

Some Tudor builders used terracotta for their most elaborate decoration. This is a kind of hard, unglazed pottery ware of much finer texture than brick. At first glance it might be mistaken for stone. Examples of its early use are seen at Layer Marney, Essex, and at Sutton Place, near Guildford, Surrey, but it never really became popular as a building material. There was a revival of its use by eighteenth- and nineteenth-century architects and obviously Ruskin approved of it when he said, 'A piece of terra cotta or plaster of Paris which has been wrought by the human hand is worth all the stone in Carrara cut by machinery', a sentiment echoed by many today as we seek to restore and preserve these interesting relics of a bygone age.

Mention should be made here of 'mathematical' tiling, which was a kind of imitation brickwork, made during the Georgian period. Hand-made and very tough, these tiles were made to hang on to an old timber house to give it a new look, or to keep out the weather. They were usually bedded on to a plaster covering but were sometimes nailed on to wooden battens, as in ordinary tile hanging. Whichever method was used they produced a smooth outer face with authentic 'bonding' to resemble brick.

There are still a number of examples to be found and when a house containing mathematical tiles is being reconditioned great care should be taken to preserve any original ones, for they are very valuable nowadays. It would be practically impossible to replace them without scouring derelict buildings.

In contrast, some people went to great lengths to disguise their bricks to the extent of facing their perfectly good brick houses with cement stucco and incising lines on to it to resemble stone blocks. Even lovely brick mouldings were often plastered in the sixteenth century to imitate stone. This practice must have been prompted by a kind of snobbery, when stone was thought to be the rich man's building material. It was the same kind of attitude which led people to have sham chimneys built. In those days the owner's social status was shown by the number of fireplaces he was able to afford, signified in turn by the number of his chimneys. The modern parallel is probably the ubiquitous television aerial.

Whatever kind of brickwork the restorer may come across he may rest assured that it can be reconditioned or, if necessary, reproduced by the specialist craftsman, using the time-honoured methods for making hand-moulded bricks. It is usually the small rural brickyard, survivor of the Industrial Revolution, that can undertake this work and fulfil all the conditions required by the most exacting client. Here the bricks are made from clay dug on their own doorstep, so to speak, well prepared and tempered to the right degree of plasticity for the job in hand.

Nowadays it would be too costly and too time-consuming to carve in the old style, so wooden moulds are used for everything; these are hand-made and capable of reproducing the most complicated ornamentation. If a piece is badly damaged there is usually enough of the original left to be used as a pattern or guide. If there isn't, a picture may be used, modelling the piece in clay from which a plaster cast is made and, finally, the wooden mould.

For example, the twisted Tudor bricks for period chimneys are made piece by piece in moulds and fitted together as the stack goes up, just as they used to be. All these the brickmaker calls 'specials'. He may also have to match up odd sizes, for until about the nineteenth century bricks varied from one part of the country to another, according to the builder's or the client's choice.

Colour is another important factor in restoration work. Old brickwork owes much of its attractiveness to differences in colour, largely because of the localized conditions in which the bricks were made, the constitution of the clay itself and the chemical action of oxides, chiefly iron or manganese, which act as staining agents. This has to be reproduced in the new bricks.

The firing is also important and the skilled craftsman knows the precise time when the bricks are sufficiently burnt to remove from the kiln.

There is a way of testing bricks by striking two together. If they produce a hard ringing sound, they are perfect. A dull, dead sound would mean that they are underburnt, or 'shuffy', as the Suffolk brickmakers say. These underfired bricks should be thrown out, for they will crumble sooner or later, and the only lasting remedy is to replace them. Occasionally it is possible to cut off about $2\frac{1}{2}$ inches of the surface and put a slip in, but it depends upon the position of the brick. Patching is a job for the expert and, generally speaking, where the amateur is up against bricks that are showing signs of crumbling, he should cut them out in their entirety and replace them with matching bricks.

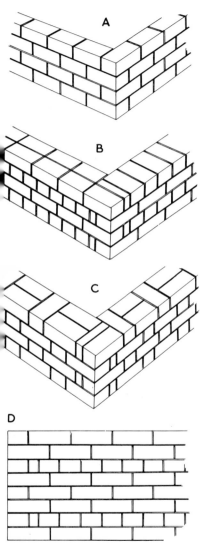

Bonding The final effect of any brickwork depends on the skill of the bricklayer, for the texture of a brick wall or a panel relies upon the composite effect of brick and the joint, which is distinguished by the technique of laying, and the bonding, that is, the manner in which the bricks are arranged.

Before the reign of Queen Anne (1702–14) they were laid in alternate courses, lengthwise, that is, with their long sides showing on the face of the wall, and across, with the end only showing: technically speaking, in headers and stretchers, which was known as the English bond. Later on, during the eighteenth century, a different method was introduced, called the Flemish bond, whereby the bricks were laid in headers and stretchers alternately in the same course, breaking up the surface still more effectively. Alternatively, they were laid in what is now known as the stretcher bond, the method used for building walls one brick thick, i.e. $4\frac{1}{2}$ inches; the English and the Flemish bonds were used in walls two or more bricks thick. Where brick panels are put in the place of wattle and daub, the use of the stretcher bond makes it possible to lay bricks without cutting them in half.

Some old cottages may be found where little or no attention has been paid to bonding patterns, with the bricks mortared together through the wall thickness, the mingled headers and stretchers interlocked to form a solid bulk. From this it can be deduced that some old-time bricklayers did not want to conform and preferred to make patterns of their own which are quite refreshing to see, particularly after looking at the dead, mechanical precision of modern brickwork.

Pointing Pointing is all important. The appearance of an old building, as well as its length of life, can be affected by bad pointing.

For all methods of bonding the joints should be in lime mortar, the whitish or creamy tint emphasizing by contrast the true colour of the brick. Repointing should be kept either flush or slightly behind the face of each brick. A slight hollowing in the joint could also be effective.

Occasionally pointing was artificially blackened, particularly in the nineteenth century when it was thought to show up the natural colour of the brick. Whether to continue this effect is a matter for the individual to decide, but generally speaking, artificially coloured pointing should not be used, unless it has been used before.

English bond looks better for fairly thick joints and a slight irregularity, but with Flemish bond regularity is important, with finer and more even joints to give a unified and balanced effect.

Fig. 7 *Patterns of brick bonding. A. Stretcher bond B. English bond C. Flemish bond D. Three-and-one bond*

Before repointing old brickwork it is important to remove all defective pointing with great care. The joints should be raked out to a depth of not less than three quarters of an inch. When the raking-out is completed all loose material should be brushed or gently washed out of the joints. This procedure is even more necessary in brickwork of the seventeenth century or later, in order not to damage the edges of fine precise work. This particularly applies to rubbed bricks which are soft and easily damaged.

Ivy roots can damage a wall by penetrating the joints and seriously weakening them. It is useless to try to pull the ivy out by the roots. They should be killed first and left to wither, then stripped off when they are dead. This is the only effective way.

It may be that a wall has been repointed comparatively recently by someone who was not familiar with the old techniques and who used hard cement. This in turn can cause strips of cement to break away from their seating, thus leaving the brickwork open for damp to penetrate the mortar underneath and the wall itself. In this case all loose pointing should be taken out and renewed with lime mortar.

The mortar mix should have a strength no greater than the strength of the walling and it should match the original weathered mortar as closely as possible. It should be remembered that pointing cannot be carried out in frosty weather, particularly with weaker mortars. Frost will kill its setting properties, and the Society for the Protection of Ancient Buildings does not recommend the use of anti-freezing agents in mortar mixes.

Incorrect pointing, or the failure to repoint when necessary, can mean seepage of moisture into the wall, with the possible result of erosion of the wall face. It can also lead to dry rot in timbers such as bonders and joist ends buried in the wall, not to mention spoiled interior decorations, and therefore the importance of good and careful pointing cannot be emphasized too strongly.

Cleaning In cleaning old brickwork, the method should be selected with great care, always taking into account the extent of the soiling. Ideally all abrasion and saturation would be excluded, but where there is heavy soiling an acid spray may be recommended, although it should be used with great caution or white, insoluble silica will be formed.

Obviously there should be a flexible approach to the choice of method since so many chemical cleaning systems are still in the experimental stages. The cautious householder may prefer to use only water and play safe, but whatever method is used all fine joints should

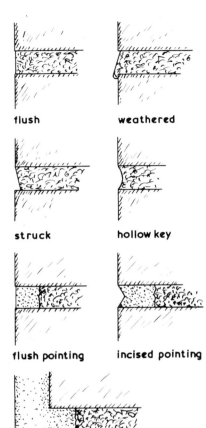

flush **weathered**

struck **hollow key**

flush pointing **incised pointing**

keyed for plaster

Fig. 8 *Jointing and pointing. The mortar between bricks may be used to finish joints or there may be a separate pointing mixture to provide a finish, where the jointing mortar is scraped out to make a key. A weathered joint is most popular for external surfaces. A struck should not be used externally as it would trap water*

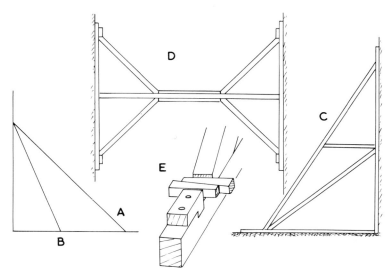

Fig. 9 *Shoring. The best support is one that applies pressure square, but if that is impossible there have to be diagonal struts. A wide angle (A) is better than a narrow one (B). There will often have to be struts at more than one level (C): brace the parts together. If something can take the load opposite, a flying shore (D) will give a direct thrust. Tightening may be against a secure block using a pair of folding wedges, driven alternately (E); then the strut should be screwed or bolted*

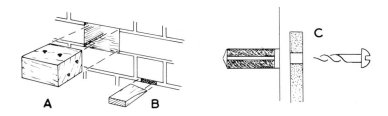

Fig. 10 *Wall fastenings. If the fixing position for something to be attached is known when a wall is being built, a piece of wood can be fitted in place of a brick. Projecting nails provide extra grip in the mortar (A). A wood plug may be cut with a twist for greater grip (B). For either plug, use a durable wood or one treated for rot resistance. If a wall is plugged for a screw, the hole should be deeper than the screw will penetrate, with the plug below the surface so that it does not lift and spread as the screw is driven (C)*

first be pointed up with non-shrink mortar. This preparation is essential before the start of any cleaning operation.

On the whole, restoring old brickwork need not present too many problems and if it is done faithfully and intelligently it will give the house its unique character as few other things will. It is often possible to find old bricks for replacement when another old building is being demolished, or they may be found in a rural builder's yard. It is worth taking the trouble to search for the right kind of bricks if you want the house to have a uniform and mellowed appearance.

Of the many types of brick houses that were built over the centuries, the Georgian house is one of the most pleasing. Eighteenth-century architecture in all its forms is the product of a highly civilized age, when there was an accepted standard of good taste, and even the smallest houses were given a simple dignity of their own.

For example, the Georgian cottage, usually of red brick – sometimes boarded – was as beautifully proportioned in its way as its grander prototypes. It had a central door with symmetrically placed windows and elliptical arches over doors and windows; these should be preserved wherever possible.

The small Georgian-type country house had a basic form which has been copied up to the present time. Again, the symmetrical façade predominates but with more emphasis on doors and on windows that have external shutters and small panes.

But the prevailing type throughout the whole century is undoubtedly the town house, or the terrace house, originally built to accommodate the needs of a large and growing middle class. The eighteenth-century builders laid out their terraces in simple, straight streets, in crescents and circuses, and splendid squares with gardens in the middle. Whichever form they took, the layout was symmetrical, but always forming vistas and avenues of masonry and brickwork, usually ending in groups of trees. It was a technique that had been copied from ancient Rome and was a complete innovation in England.

Nevertheless, this meticulous planning was not reserved for the wealthy but was for all classes to enjoy. It has been said that in no other country in the world has such a large section of its community been housed in such dignity. This is why it is so gratifying that so many of these lovely houses, both large and small, are being restored to their former elegance.

Of course, town planning of this sort would not have been possible if every man had built his own house. What happened was that the

6   *Newly restored brick wall at Trinity Hospital, Long Melford, Suffolk. The original Tudor bricks were made in the sixteenth century and have been copied; they were made by hand and pointed in period style by a local brickmaker*

original owner of the land 'developed' it as a speculation, and tenants paid suitable rents.

Four architects, the two Woods and the two Dances, both fathers and sons, developed large areas of Bath and Dublin respectively, while later on in the century the Adam brothers developed still more of Georgian London and introduced a style quite their own. By this time the design of terrace houses was so standardized that it is only in the general layout and the details that there is any change in style.

Basically, it was the density of houses towards the end of the seventeenth century that gave rise to the invention of the terrace as a means of preserving the status of the occupant together with economy in space. By building a whole street of houses all run together and treated as an architectural whole, small houses could be given all the dignity of a mansion.

These terraces took the form of simple brick buildings usually topped by a parapet, or cornice, which concealed a shallow, sloping roof. In clay districts the houses were invariably of brick, but in stone areas, such as Bath, the local material was used. There were thick walls between the houses, which served the dual purpose of preventing fire from spreading from one house to the next, and carrying the chimney stacks, which were made as unobtrusive as possible.

The standard details of these houses are a familiar sight in almost any town. The buildings are usually four storeys high, with a short flight of steps up to the front door. There is a basement below the ground floor, with the principal rooms on the first floor, and the whole façade is dignified by the most beautifully proportioned windows that have ever been seen. It was the age when the sash window was first introduced and the Georgian builders made them tall and stately-looking, with delicate wooden glazing bars in standard-sized panes of glass. The basic plan was to have short windows on the ground floor for solidity, very tall windows on the first floor for grandeur, slightly shorter ones on the next, and at the top of the house, completely square windows to serve as a kind of full stop. It was a subtle design in which the architects excelled.

The front doors are usually of generous size, panelled, with semi-circular fanlights over them. Inside, a rectangular or oval stone staircase leads upwards, balustraded in fine wrought iron, in accordance with the size of the house.

Of course, the Adam brothers, whose terrace houses are among the most delightful in the country, refined all the Georgian features of a town house, taking their inspiration from ancient Greece. They used the Greek honeysuckle pattern freely – in plasterwork, on columns and in the fine wrought-ironwork of balconies, in ceilings and in the decorations over chimneypieces. This delicate use of ornament, of garlands, urns and paterae, was scornfully dismissed by Horace Walpole as 'all gingerbread, filigraine and fan-painting', but despite this sour remark by a testy old gentleman, the Adam brothers exercised a widespread influence during the late eighteenth century and their work is still highly prized today.

Anyone wishing to restore a Georgian house of this type cannot do better than visit one of the houses that are open to the public. There is a splendid example of a late eighteenth-century house in Bristol, at 7 Great George Street. The façade is of Bath stone, well proportioned and somewhat austere-looking, but inside are all the classical features that one has come to expect from an age devoted to the famous Adams.

Another house that is typical of its time is to be seen at 1 Royal Crescent, Bath. It was beautifully restored in 1968 by Bernard Cayzer, who presented it to the Bath Preservation Trust. The first and second floors of the house are furnished exactly as they would have been in the eighteenth century and everything is correct down to the smallest detail.

Few people would dispute the case for restoration where these elegant houses are concerned, and it is heartening to see in our large towns whole areas where they are being given new life. This applies particularly to those parts of London where there is much beautiful, though neglected, Georgian building.

Two examples epitomize the types discussed here. One is in the heart of London's Mayfair, an area which once saw better days. This lovely house has now been bought by a commercial organization for use as combined residential and office accommodation, and it has been so well restored that one can imagine the Regency dandies and their ladies who no doubt lived in it at one time.

Externally, the front elevation is of Portland stone with a roof covered in Westmorland slate. Slender iron railings at street level are complemented by a graceful wrought-iron balcony to the first floor (Plate 7). At the rear is a courtyard laid in random York stone paving, which makes a delightful small walled garden. All of this was renewed and brought back to the original.

Inside, the house had been neglected and needed complete refurbishing. The most impressive feature in the entrance hall is the open staircase sweeping in wide curves from the ground to the third floor (Plate 8). This had a fine wrought-iron balustrade with a

7 *Exterior of a newly restored Georgian house in Mayfair, London*

polished mahogany handrail terminating in a scroll. Some of the
wrought-ironwork was damaged, with delicate leaves and scrolls
rusted or broken, and these were renewed by skilled craftsmen so well
that it is impossible to see where the damage was. The original
mahogany panelled front door, with the semi-circular fanlight, was
missing, with some nondescript substitute put in its place (Plate 9).
The door has now been replaced in the form it would have taken when

8   *Entrance hall of Mayfair
house after restoration, with
period front door and fanlight
reinstated*

9 Entrance hall of Mayfair house before restoration (Morgan Wells Studio)

the house was built, the white shutters were reinstated at the windows, marble was laid on the floor, the plaster cornice and ceiling were renewed by craftsmen, and the panelled walls restored and repainted. A chandelier gives the final touch of elegance to this very beautiful entrance hall, which, indeed, sets the scene for the rest of the house, for the same pattern has been followed in all the rooms. Where modern amenities have been installed, such as central heating and an

automatic lift, they have been done so unobtrusively that one has
to search for them.

Altogether this is a totally sympathetic refurbishment, and one
hopes that this trend will continue to develop among the commercial
houses, for it would do much to save the larger buildings which the
ordinary householder could not hope to restore.

On a considerably smaller scale is a similar type of late eighteenth-
century terrace house in Islington, a London borough which is rich in
this kind of property and where much is now being done to conserve
it. This house is in red brick and follows the usual pattern of four
storeys, with a short flight of steps to the front door and a semi-
basement. The exterior is unremarkable (Plate 10), but the real beauty
and sheer grace of the house is apparent the moment the front door is
opened and one sees the extent of the work that has been done, and the
care that has been taken to keep it in period.

Downstairs, the basement room overlooks the front garden and
was probably once the domain of servants. This has been made into a
formal dining room, with the open fireplace fully restored with all
period furnishings, including a brass dog grate and an Adam-style
chimneypiece delicately carved with the typical designs of urns and
paterae. In the recesses each side of the fireplace are built-in display
cupboards which house some special household treasures, and the
plaster cornice, in simple Greek key pattern, has been restored, all
fully in keeping with the architecture. The floor was relaid with solid
concrete and damp-proofed, then overlaid with wood blocks, partially covered with a large square rug. Leaving an area of polished
wood flooring uncovered like this makes a perfect setting for fine
mahogany furniture, all in period.

At the back of the dining room is the new kitchen, which makes no
pretence of being anything but modern with up-to-date fitments. It is
panelled in pine and the general effect is one of muted efficiency. A
further extension was built on to take a utility room and a shower
room, but this was the only structural alteration that took place, apart
from the comparatively simple one of turning the stairs. These
originally led straight into the kitchen, which was a great incon-
venience. Now they have been turned to terminate in the hall – a much
better arrangement from all standpoints. Part of the old staircase was
too worn to be reused, so the owner sent these parts to a joiner with
instructions to copy them exactly. The result is excellent.

The kitchen has a surprisingly beautiful outlook to an old walled
garden, 100 feet long but only 17 feet wide. In order to make the most
of this long, narrow plot, the owners built a low brick wall with a

10 *Eighteenth-century town
house in Islington, London,
restored true to type*

wrought-iron gate set within an arch, half-way down the garden, so that the garden beyond this point is seen as a vista. One or two old trees, a small lily pool, a rock garden and well laid out borders complete what is an amazingly peaceful oasis in the heart of a busy city street.

On the ground floor, just above street level, is the drawing room, traditional in every sense except that the division between two small rooms, once separated by folding doors, is now curtained with sleek velvet hangings on heavy brass rings and curtain pole. In this room the oak panelling has been perfectly restored and matched, with specially run mouldings around the panels. The wood has been so well cut and placed that not a join shows anywhere. Built-in bookcases at one end make the most of all available space. The fireplace has also been restored in this room and open fires are enjoyed on winter evenings, probably just as they would have been two hundred years ago.

On the first floor is the principal bedroom, a light, airy room with white-painted shutters on the inside of the long windows. A connecting door to a dressing room has been effectively concealed by taking away the architraves and making it flush with the wall, with an unobtrusive drop ring handle to open it. A mirror on the wall completes the illusion. In these rooms new polished pine floorboards were put down, with rugs here and there for comfort.

On the floor above are two more large rooms, one of which is used for a study, well away from the domestic scene. Everywhere one is struck by the space, an impression which is somewhat belied by the outside appearance of the house, but that is the beauty of a true Georgian town house. There is ample room for cupboards, two bathrooms and all the usual additions we have come to expect in these twentieth-century days, which, of course, includes central heating made as unobtrusive as possible. I have seldom seen so perfect an example of restoration and refurbishing, from the furniture and furnishings down to the last finger plates and escutcheons in neo-classical style. It is the outcome of much careful research and insistence on attention to detail by the owners. Even the glazing bars on the windows had to be the right thickness, for this house was built at the end of the eighteenth century when glazing bars were even thinner than previously. It is immensely rewarding to see the results of such meticulous restoration, and although it was not quite complete when I saw it, it held promise of sheer perfection.

11 *Interior of Islington house, with two rooms made into one by the removal of doors*

4
The Stone House

The possessor of a stone house rightly feels that he has a home of solidity and permanence, the rock-like quality of its stout walls imparting a sense of security unrivalled by any other kind of building. True, it is well-nigh impermeable, but like any other natural material, stone needs care to prevent it decaying.

There is, of course, a tremendous variation in building stone, ranging from the flints and chalks of East Anglia and the sandstones of parts of the Midlands and Yorkshire, to the granites of the north and west, with a great belt of limestone in between, running through Dorset, east Somerset, Gloucestershire, north Wiltshire, Oxfordshire, Northampton, Leicestershire and Nottinghamshire to east Yorkshire; it is this limestone which produces some of the finest building material in the world and, not surprisingly, a great tradition has grown up around it. This is particularly noticeable in the Cotswolds.

At one time stone was the rich man's building material, mainly because of the difficulties of transporting it to the site. It was taken by ship from coastal quarries, up the rivers and overland by packhorse, if need be, but somehow it got there, and the results still survive in many an old castle and keep. We may still find a small stone house here and there, the relic of a medieval manor house, the timber hall which once stood beside it long since gone. It was not until much later, from the time of the Renaissance onwards, that stone came within the reach of the ordinary middle-class person. Now, in these days of technological wonders, we are in danger of ignoring it or, at best, debasing it, and building in stone is becoming increasingly rare except in those districts where the local material is readily available.

Today the stonemason is more often called upon to restore old buildings than to put up new ones, and it is in this field of restoration that the rural mason excels. Usually he comes from a long line of craftsmen, inheriting a deep-rooted pride in his ancient trade. He knows his material intimately and understands the peculiar characteristics of each type of stone – its texture, its colour and the special techniques required to work it to the best advantage. In short, he has an affinity with his craft which few others share, or even understand. In effect, the master mason must combine a practical knowledge of geology with the science of building, for he works in close co-operation with architects and is frequently consulted by them. Indeed, the fourteenth-century stonemason was virtually an architect, an essential and important member of the community, and his skills were widely recognized then, as now.

The art of quarrying and stone dressing is an ancient one, practised by the Romans and the Normans to a high degree of efficiency and with much the same kind of tools that are in use today. It is impossible to follow, within the compass of this book, all the methods involved in shaping and dressing the different kinds of stone, for in the past they varied from district to district. For example, the harder stones, such as

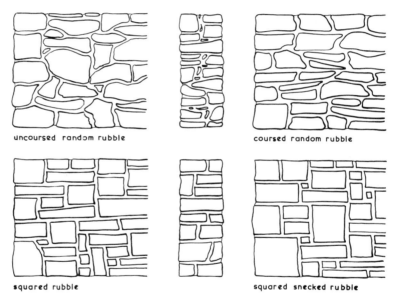

uncoursed random rubble   coursed random rubble

squared rubble   squared snecked rubble

Fig. 11 *Masonry walls. Stone walls may be made with random rubble with no attempt at forming courses, or the stones may be chosen to form some courses along the wall. Squared stones may be laid in a similar way, or a pattern can be built up by snecking. Snecks are the small square-ended stones used to bring joints between stones of random sizes into line. The pattern may be on the surface only, with waste stone filling the centre, although the wall is stronger if opposing stones are fitted and some go right through*

Cornish granites, were dressed with a heavy scabbling hammer (a sledge hammer with a pointed head) to take off irregular angles, and were then tooled with chisels. Softer stone, such as Bath stone, could be dressed with combs. Purbeck stone required wedges and a hammer to cut it, and an experienced eye was needed to find the exact place for splitting. These are just random examples but they suffice to show that the restoration of old stonework is, generally speaking, a job for a skilled stonemason. He knows well the individual properties of each kind of stone, and the correct way to treat it when it falls into disrepair.

Having stressed the enduring qualities of stone, what then is likely to cause its deterioration? There are, in fact, a number of factors.

The stone may be worn by friction – by wind erosion – and this is most marked in exposed situations where the building is unprotected in any way. There may be damage by frost, again in exposed situations. Freezing water in the pores of stone, which are not sufficiently big to allow for the expansion of ice, will disrupt and burst the stone in the same way that ice will burst a water pipe. Also, rainwater can wash out the mortar from the joints, and as it expands into ice, it will force them apart. A damp, unventilated place will cause trouble, too. Mossy patches, efflorescence and other staining indicate the presence of dampness and this should be traced to its source and rectified without delay. A wall must be protected at its base against ground moisture.

In one case, in Scotland, the excessive dampness was traced to a faulty damp-proof course. The owner cured the trouble by digging a trench all round the house (a detached one) to a depth of 2 feet, painting the walls below ground level with bitumen paint to make a membrane, then filling in with stone chips, rather like railway ballast, and covering the surface with fine chips for decorative reasons. In this instance it was a very effective remedy but, of course, all cases have to be judged individually, taking into account the cause of the dampness.

By far the greatest enemy of a stone building is atmospheric pollution, i.e., soot deposits, sulphur gases and the like, which will gradually eat into the stone, causing untold damage. Aesthetically, dirt not only disfigures and masks the colour and character of different stones and blurs ornamental detail but it does something potentially more dangerous when it hides open joints and structural faults such as cracking. This is far more likely to occur in towns than in rural areas where the air is cleaner. Another reason for the deterioration in some stones is the careless or ignorant selection at the quarry in the first place. This is a failing to which the Victorians were prone. For instance, pure sandstone, being chemically inert, can withstand the pollution of a smoke-laden atmosphere much better than a limestone and is therefore better for industrial areas. There are many other reasons for the careful selection of stone in given situations, but these are too technical to pursue here in detail.

Another common failing of the Victorian builders was the use of iron clamps in masonry, which rusted and destroyed the stone. They used them mostly to hold Bath stone in place, which is very soft, instead of using sufficient mortar to bind the stones together. The result, in some cases, has been disastrous. The only remedy is to cut out the damaged stone and replace it with new stone of the original type. If this proves to be impossible to obtain, then a little care should be taken to ensure that replacement stones are at least of the same geological type and appearance, so that they match and will weather down in time to blend in with the old. Needless to say, patching with cement is abhorrent and ruins the appearance of a building. It is just as cheap to cut out a decayed part and put in new stone as it is to patch, and it is much more satisfactory in every way.

At the same time, it is important to avoid a patchy effect, even with new stone. The old masons aimed at precision in contours and alignment but did not overdo the finish. Ashlar (stonework dressed to a fine surface) looks too mechanical if 'dragged' with a comb, or rubbed, and natural weathering may be prevented. This is important to remember where new stone is being introduced to combine with old which already has a texture and colour mellowed by time. The skilled mason will leave new stone 'from the tool', so that it gets a little dust on it and soon looks old. Other kinds of masonry should follow the customs of the district, the 'hammer dressed' or 'chopped' faces being made as accurate as the tool permits. Even where the material is rough, coursing should be level, and no stones should be set sloping one way or the other to disturb the eye. Wherever possible, the original joint pattern should be continued.

Building an extension in stone is a job that calls for considerable expertise. I saw an extension being built to a large eighteenth-century lodge in a village near Gloucester. The original is a substantial building in classical style and the three large rooms and bathroom being thrown out from it so totally merge with the old lodge that it will be difficult to detect the new work once the stone has weathered down. Every detail has been faithfully copied, down to the miniature balustrading round the parapet of the roof. New building like this requires its own brand of skill, for the mason, unlike the bricklayer, has to prepare his own blocks of stone to conform with the original. The heavy stone slabs are bonded together with mason's putty – a mixture of lime, white cement and stone dust in correct proportions, the ideal being that the crushing strength of the cement is the same as the crushing strength of the stone. The work has to be exact; there is no margin for error.

Pointing   As with brickwork pointing is all-important and will make or mar the appearance of a building as well as its durability. The joints of ashlar should not be emphasized in any way, either by raising them or sinking them, or by the use of coloured mortar. They should be fine enough to be virtually invisible, and great care should be taken not to increase the width of the joint when repointing.

With rubble stone (unsquared or undressed stone) the thickness of the mortar bed will inevitably be larger; nevertheless, the technique is the same, i.e. to emphasize the stone more than the pointing, and this is done by recessing the pointing slightly to bring out the stone's shape and character and by giving the mortar a colour and texture as near to that of the stone as possible, to avoid its being conspicuous.

There may be some local circumstances or traditions which should be taken into account, and it is as well to respect these in new pointing; but on the whole, the above methods are acceptable. The mortar should always be softer than the stones and a soft lime mix is recommended. Basically, the mortar is made up of coarse sand which at one time was mixed with slaked lime, although nowadays Portland cement is used. The colour of the mortar is governed by the choice of sand but, generally speaking, the mix for every job should be decided individually since, chemically, the composition of the mortar should vary according to the nature of the stone to which it is being applied.

Before repointing, any old crumbling mortar must be raked out thoroughly; then pointing up is done with a trowel. When all the mortar is dried out the surface is scratched off and finished with a brush to remove all cement dust.

Cleaning   Stone buildings improve with natural weathering which helps them to merge with their environment, but that does not mean that they should be left to sink into a state of decay.

The surface of stone may be protected to a limited extent by the use of silicones. A light coating of one of the recommended solutions will help to avert the decay caused by lichens clinging to the stone (though the lichens themselves may look very pleasing), but the building should first be cleaned down to remove all harmful grime.

Stonemasons who specialize in restoration work recommend

nothing but the use of a fine water spray. Anything else may be actively harmful. Some public bodies advise the use of acid sprays, which at first sight may appear to do the job well but which in fact result in the breaking down of the cementation of the grains of the stone and so hasten the process of decay. Likewise, sand blasting, now a popularly advertised process, is good for nothing but sandstones or granites because it destroys the natural protective callus that forms on the stone after the quarry sap has dried out of it. This leaves it vulnerable to the effects of rain, which is in itself a weak acid. Water cleaning gets down to the callus but does not destroy it; the callus will stay there for hundreds of years if left undisturbed. Sand blasting may better be used for the inside of a building, but it is still not good for the stone. It follows that after such drastic treatment the softer material of joints will be liable to break down, and in less than twenty years the stone itself will start flaking.

For different reasons, stone should not be painted. It is a natural material and needs to breathe, and paint will soon flake off. Also, if water gets behind the paint, it will accelerate the decay.

The ordinary householder will do well to stick to the safe method of water cleaning for old stonework, using only fine sprays and non-ferrous wire brushes or bristle brushes to brush out the more inaccessible parts. Sometimes a little hand rubbing with abrasive stones also helps. Any thick deposits of soot can be lifted away with a wooden scraper. Great care should be taken not to remove more than the surface grime and so spoil the patina of age which lies underneath it. Neither is it necessary to scrub out every tiny particle of dirt from carvings and ornamentation. More harm than good may be done by too drastic treatment and a wealth of interesting detail may be lost.

Washing should be done when there is no likelihood of frost, and care should be taken to prevent water penetrating inside the house. It is advisable to shield windows and doors with polythene sheeting and if the house is on the public highway the public must be protected from possible hazards. All necessary precautions to prevent accidents must be taken when any kind of exterior work is being done. Another useful point to bear in mind is that aluminium ladders, being springy and fairly sharp, are likely to mark stonework unless they are protected.

Inside the house a different method must be used. Old stonework, such as that around fireplaces, can be scrubbed clean with mild soap and water, and when dry, a colourless wax polish can be brushed into it, taking care not to leave any surplus on the stone. This can be followed by a light coat of colourless liquid vinyl polish, buffed well as soon as it dries. This helps to seal the more porous stones and gives a pleasing, smooth finish, easy to keep clean.

Having generalized thus far and passed on advice from a craftsman stonemason, it is only fair to add that with the new cleaning techniques that are developing today a more flexible approach to the choice of materials may be required in the future. When the existence of a very old historic building is at stake the Society for the Protection of Ancient Buildings is always pleased to advise and answer queries.

Repairing stonework   An old house of any period from Tudor times onwards may well contain some beautiful carved stonework. Fireplaces, in particular, were often singled out for special treatment, probably because the fire, with its friendly, cheerful blaze, was the central point of hospitality and so it also became the focal point of decoration to which all eyes would turn on entering a room. It is still so today and many restorers are actively engaged in replacing what an undiscriminating predecessor has tried to destroy. The question of repairing or replacing decorative stonework, either inside or outside the house, is one and the same. In short, it is a job for the master craftsman, one who is skilled in carving and knows his material well. The technique includes matching up the original stone as well as matching up the detail, so that when it is weathered down the new merges with the old without jarring. I saw a perfect example of this technique in a restored window at Tewkesbury, Gloucestershire. New stone mullions and transoms had been made which were identical to the original. Only a slight difference in the look of the new stone was apparent and this would vanish in another few weeks. Had anyone but a skilled craftsman done this work it would merely have looked an eyesore.

Many people believe that building in stone or restoring stone is too expensive for the average householder to consider, but this is a fallacy. When I consulted a stonemason he told me, 'A mason's work is much cheaper than people think. The cost of stone compares very favourably with other materials nowadays, and if the public would only ask for prices they would realize the truth of this.' It is a good point to remember for anyone who is involved in restoring a stone house.

Reconstituted stone   There is another method of restoring ornamental stonework and garden statuary – by using reconstituted stone. There is nothing new about this. Landscape gardeners and architects have used it since the late eighteenth century, but it is now, in a sense, being 'rediscovered'. It is, quite simply, ground-down stone mixed with a little water and a little cement, and the resulting product is hard to distinguish from its natural counterpart, although, of course, the secret of success lies with the nature of the ingredients, the correct proportions used and the final mix. Very often years of study and experiment have gone into the making of the kind of reconstituted stone which is judged to be the right medium for restoration purposes; this has a soft composition which encourages the growth of lichen and mosses, so that it mellows quickly. It also withstands frost and extremes of weather, which makes it ideal for out-of-doors work.

The technique for restoring broken ornamentation in reconstituted stone is the same as that for other similar media. A pattern is made of the broken or missing pieces, from which a mould is made. Sometimes the craftsman has nothing but old prints or photographs to go on when he is looking for details of the original; in these cases he has to make scale drawings and create his own clay model from which a rubber mould is made. Both of these processes are considerable feats of expertise in themselves when one considers some of the difficult and intricate details that have to be reproduced when copying classical figures and embellishments. The final stage is to pack the rubber mould with stone dust, ramming it down tightly so that pressure is even over the entire surface and no flaws or air pockets are left to spoil the shape of the finished object. After it has been wetted and left out of doors to set it still has to be finished by hand to give it a fine sculptured look.

Though these craftsmen are in demand by the National Trust, the Department of the Environment and similar public bodies, they are still able and willing to take on a one-off job for the ordinary householder. It may be a stone moulding that needs replacing; a piece of a balustrade broken off; or a broken ornament on a gate-post – all things that can be found in a Georgian house, things that give it its gracious character and a touch of real beauty.

Statuary and garden stonework   Landscape and setting enhance the beauty of any house, small or large. During the last century the architects of the Arts and Crafts movement sought to integrate house and garden, so that one complemented the other, and it is still a good rule to follow whenever practicable. A well-chosen piece of statuary can be used as a focal point to draw attention to some particularly beautiful climbing plants, for example, or a background of natural, graceful trees – *not* those poor tortured shapes that have been ruthlessly 'cut back' without regard to their nature, but those that have been shaped and balanced, to look as Nature meant them to look. Obviously the way statuary and other stonework is used in a garden must depend upon individual judgement, but it should never be allowed to become overpowering.

Dry stone walls　Building a dry stone wall is not a difficult task for the handyman to tackle, which is fortunate since dry stone wallers, as craftsmen, are very hard to find these days.

In many parts of the country, such as the Dales of Yorkshire, the Cotswolds and North Wales, dry stone walls are part of the landscape and their repair, or renewal, is vital to the general scheme of house and garden.

Although no mortar or cement is used in the building of these walls, they have to be solid enough to withstand the force of winds and storms in exposed places. The art arises in the ability to work with irregular-size stones, assessing the possibility of each one and knowing whether it will fit into a particular gap. Large regular stones are laid in a way that provides a solid base for the wall and thereafter it is built up methodically, with a line of tie stones – stones laid lengthways in the form of a bond – inserted when the wall is built up

12　*Building a dry stone wall. A free-standing wall should be twice as thick at the bottom as at the top*

to half its final height. In addition to large stones, smaller ones are inserted in the body of the wall to fill all spaces. The top is levelled with large flat stones and the coping is completed by using pointed or rounded stones placed on edge at the top of the wall.

This is just a generalization of the method used, since in this, as in so many other country crafts, local customs vary, and it is up to the individual to observe what has been done before and to do likewise.

Flint Flint houses are fairly common in the south-east of England. There was a great revival of flint-faced building during the Regency and Victorian periods, particularly in those counties south of the Thames – Kent, Surrey and Sussex – and a good deal is still to be found in Berkshire and Hampshire. It is these houses, with their solid walls and sturdy construction, that respond so well to restoration, for flint is a notoriously hard-wearing stone, virtually indestructible, yet it can be split to make a brilliant-looking building stone. Only a skilled flint-knapper knows how to cut or 'knap' a quarried stone along its planes of weakness, so that it shows its black inner face. In some cases the stones are left rough, but the best flints are black and very hard, while the inferior stuff tends to be greyer and more brittle.

Whole flints had to be bedded in a great deal of mortar, and it followed that the ultimate strength of the wall depended upon the nature of the mortar. In restoring a flint-faced wall it is essential, therefore, to get the right mixture of mortar, which should be soft, in order to bed down the hard flints successfully. Individual flints are not difficult to replace, but where a large area of mortar needs to be covered, such as in the joints, it can be galleted very effectively with small pieces of flint or stone. (Galleting means inserting tiny pieces of stone or flint into mortar while it is still soft. It can be very decorative.) It is much better than leaving an unsightly patch of mortar just as it is.

When properly constructed, a flint-faced building will stand up to the weather much better than many varieties of stone, as witness the many old flint barns one sees dotted around the countryside, particularly in Sussex, a number of which have now been successfully converted into comfortable houses.

Victorian schools, no longer suitable for their original purpose, are also being rescued from the bulldozer by enterprising people, their great advantage being the large and lofty rooms which lend themselves to many purposes. For example, The Old School, Clanfield, Hampshire, is one that has been restored and converted recently after a good deal of hard work on the part of the owners. Built in 1857, it was first a village school for thirty-six pupils and later did

duty as a church hall, before being sold to a private buyer who saw all its possibilities as a home with a difference.

With walls of solid, irregularly shaped flints on a brick foundation, a steeply pitched red-tiled roof with high, pointed gables, it is listed as 'a Hampshire Treasure' and must not be altered in appearance externally. No such restrictions were placed on the interior, however, and planning permission was easy to obtain, enabling the new owners to move in as quickly as possible to begin work on the restoration. The original building consisted of one large schoolroom with a later, smaller one built on at the back in brick, faced with flints, and a small lobby where the children used to hang their coats. A cottage next-door was the schoolmaster's house, with two up and two down and a very steep staircase in the middle. It was decided to use the cottage

13 *The Old School, Clanfield, Hampshire, its exterior unaltered after restoration. The old school bell remains in the gable*

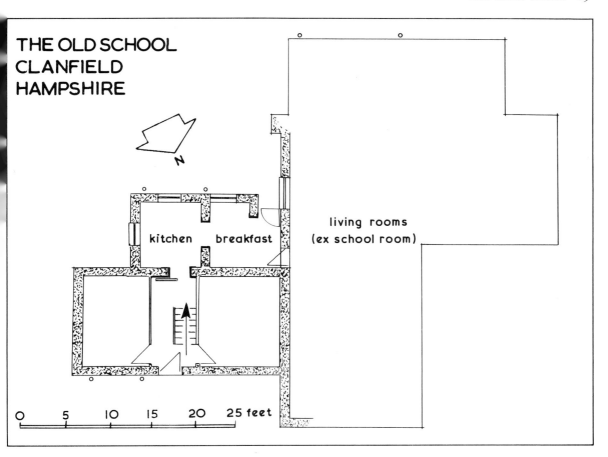

**THE OLD SCHOOL
CLANFIELD
HAMPSHIRE**

N

kitchen   breakfast

living rooms
(ex school room)

O   5   10   15   20   25 feet

Fig. 12 *Plan of The Old School,
Clanfield, Hampshire*

entirely as bedrooms with a bathroom, and to build on an extension at
the back comprising a kitchen and a breakfast room to make a link
between the cottage and the school. It puts the new kitchen in the
middle of the house with access to both parts – a very convenient
arrangement.

Some old outhouses had to be demolished to make room for a
brick-built garage, but there was no other demolition and the whole
conversion has been done on a shoestring.

To buy the property a mortgage was arranged with a building
society, who stipulated that all treatment for woodworm (there were
one or two rotten joists) and a silicone injection damp-proof course
should be done by a specialist firm who would give a guarantee. Apart
from that, it was an exercise in do-it-yourself from start to finish.

Getting rid of the effects of neglected damp was a major problem, which necessitated stripping walls of decaying plaster and treating them with a damp-proof compound before replastering. Ceilings in the cottage had to be ripped out in order to replace the rotten joists, and several sash windows also had to be replaced, all in character with the Victorian building, and painted white. Wallpapers for the cottage were carefully chosen and kept in period.

The roof was partially retiled, using as many as possible of the original tiles, and the whole was insulated with glass fibre. Since the main door to the big schoolroom was no longer needed (the front door of the cottage is now the main entrance), it was filled in and replaced with an arched window, to match the others.

The big schoolroom has been left just as it was to make a magnificent all-purpose sitting room, its high, vaulted, wooden ceiling adding to the general feeling of light and space. The old Victorian flap ventilators at ceiling height were taken out as being too draughty and more modern ones installed, but all the old joinery was left intact, including the capacious schoolroom cupboards, which give excellent storage space. The floors were solid 1-inch boards and the flint walls were so hard that it was difficult to find a place to drive a nail without exploring for a space between the flints, but it is this very solidity that makes a flint house so warm and cosy to live in. There is a fireplace at each end of this big room, both of which burn well and give a cheerful blaze when needed. In fact, all the other rooms in the cottage have their Victorian fireplaces, many with their original tiles and distinctive grates, although in addition, there is gas central heating, an unobtrusive modern convenience. Two systems were installed, one for the cottage and another for the schoolrooms, kitchen and breakfast room, with plentiful hot water always available. The smaller schoolroom is now a splendid playroom, with very little alteration needed. It leads off an entrance lobby with a cloakroom alongside. This neatly confines muddy garden boots and playtime activities to one section of the house at the back.

It took a year's hard work to get the place in order, but in spite of the inevitable chaos the owners are glad they moved in straight away, because they changed their minds about siting some things more than once before they found the perfect solution.

They went to immense trouble to keep the house in period, even to

14   *The schoolroom, The Old School, transformed into a pleasant sitting room with a dining area just visible in the foreground*

leaving the old school bell where it has been since the place was built, high up in the gable above the big schoolroom. It is still rung on ceremonial occasions, the last of which was the wedding of TRH The Prince and Princess of Wales, when the village children eagerly took a hand in clanging it out once more.

Cob   Although, strictly speaking, cob is not in the category of stone, it is one of the oldest building materials, seen a good deal in the West Country where it has a very strong tradition. It has been described as a 'lump' walling material, hence its name. Basically, it is mud or clay, or chalk mixed with gravel and bound together with straw, which is then plastered over. The plaster builds up a durable skin and prevents disintegration.

Proof of the durability of cob walls is seen in Sir Walter Raleigh's house, Hayes Barton, a cob and thatch farmhouse in the Otter Valley. Built in Elizabethan days, it is one of south Devon's great attractions, and is in a fine state of preservation. It looks as if its sturdy cob walls will endure for ever.

Cob is not difficult to repair. It is usually the plaster rendering that cracks or bulges, with the consequent danger of letting the rain in to the wall beneath. Any bulging patches of plaster or loose flakings should be prised clear of the cob, as should any cracked or crumbling material from around doors, windows, etc. Then one should use a soft-setting cement and plaster over the bare patches, making sure that it is worked well into the edges all round. Trowel it to an even thickness so that it blends in with the wall, and the job is done. The same treatment applies to interior cob walls that are plastered over in the same way. A little unevenness or undulation in the walls does not matter in the least; in fact, it adds to the 'home-spun' look of the building, which is part of the charm of cob.

Roughcast and pebble-dash   In Britain roughcast often provides a covering for rubblestone masonry of all kinds, or it may be used to disguise inferior brickwork. It is, briefly, a wet mixture of cement and small stones thrown on to an external wall covering of cement and sand before the backing coat has dried. Pebble-dash is the form in which small stones or pebbles are thrown on to a rendered wall when wet without being mixed with cement. It is a cheap and easy way of protecting a wall, but not always attractive. In Scotland roughcast is known as harling, and it is much more highly regarded than it is in England, with great importance placed on the quality of the material and the method of mixing and applying. Both roughcast and pebble-dash are generally supposed to give soft and porous stone additional protection against the weather, but it is a question of preference as to which method is used. If too much cement is used in roughcast it can be visually ugly, and if pieces drop off it allows the water to penetrate behind them. It is not easy to patch without the result showing and the most satisfactory way is to complete a whole wall in one operation.

A successful and pleasing example of Scottish harling is seen on The Old Smithy at Gartocharn where part of the restoration consisted of roughcasting the old stone walls and painting them white with Weathershield.

The old building, long since discarded as a smithy, is about two hundred years old, but it was still serviceable. A husband and wife, with two young sons, saw in it the home they needed, so they sold a car to get a bridging loan which enabled them to buy it. They also had

15 *The Old Smithy, Gartocharn, Dunbartonshire, as it was nearly two hundred years ago*

a grant from the local authority, which was a considerable help. They consulted an architect who drew up plans, and these were duly passed in accordance with the Town and Country Planning Act, after which the young couple set to work doing everything themselves, with the plans to guide them and the architect to advise. They built walls of thermalite partitions to divide the building into one large living room, with a kitchen thrown out at the back, an entrance hall and linen cupboard, four bedrooms and a bathroom. Although the original smithy was sizeable, it would only take two bedrooms, but there was enough land at the side of it to take an extension for the two remaining bedrooms, so that two growing boys could each have a room, with a spare room for guests. The extension is so well done that it looks like a part of the original building, both inside and out. In fact, it is hard to imagine this trim, well-planned house ever having been used for such a rural occupation as shoeing horses, or that the old anvil once stood on the site of the living room, now a very pleasant family room. Here the original windows were kept, with deep sills built into the 30-inch-thick cavity walls. At the opposite end of the room, french windows lead out to a small paved terrace and a garden. Softwood beams, stained and varnished, support the roof joists, which had to be renewed, along with the rafters, but the dominating feature of this room is a large, red, sandstone fireplace, built along the external wall. This contains a well-designed wood-burning stove which operates radiators for central heating as well as supplying domestic hot water, and this, with the thick outer walls, keeps the house warm and cosy through the long winters.

The principal bedroom occupies the space where the horses used to stand, waiting their turn to be shod, and this, too, has its original windows.

As one would expect, the original floors were just beaten earth with sleepers laid on them, but they are now covered with chipboard on joists, and in the case of the entrance hall and the new kitchen they are vinyl tiled. The kitchen also has a pine-boarded ceiling and pine-faced units, thoroughly up to date in every detail, but the rest of the house is painted white, with wallpapers and soft furnishings most carefully chosen in keeping with the style of house.

The entire roof was reslated with slates on sarking (thin boards) lined with breathable felt, then insulated with glass fibre. The slates were second-hand, obtained from an old byre on a nearby farm, so they are genuinely local. In this and every other respect, the owners have been at pains to make the old smithy blend in with other houses in the neighbourhood, and they have succeeded magnificently. The

Fig. 13   *Plan of The Old Smithy, Gartocharn, Dunbartonshire*

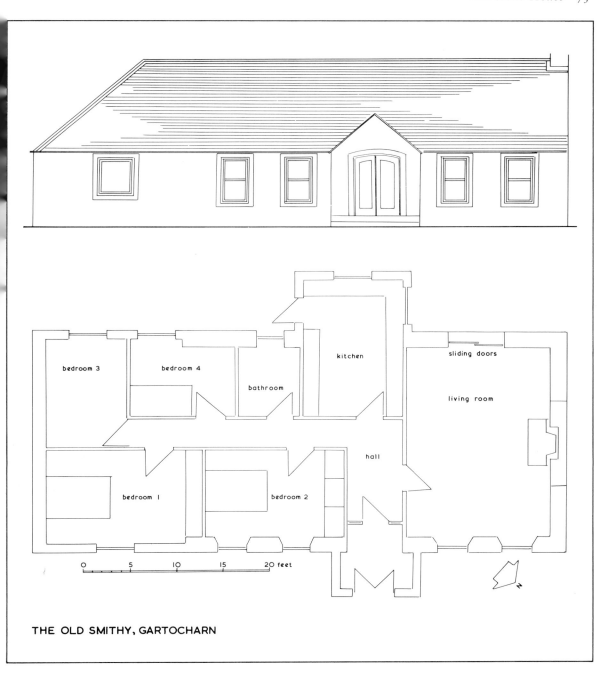

THE OLD SMITHY, GARTOCHARN

final touch was the building of a dry stone wall along the front garden, with old stones that were left over from other work.

Incredibly, the work took only fifteen months from start to finish – and that was working in spare time – and it was achieved on a very low budget. As an example of single-minded enthusiasm it is surely hard to beat. It is also an example of the many instances I found of the friendly co-operation between architect and client.

At the other end of the scale, also in Scotland, I saw a castle, occupying the summit of a rocky knoll overlooking Ardmaddy Bay in Argyllshire. It was a beautiful place for a young man to inherit, bound up with Scottish history and happy family memories, but impossible to restore and keep up by modern standards. The answer to the problem came, in this case, by demolishing a Victorian wing which had been added to the old building during the nineteenth century and

16 *The Old Smithy, as it is today, with the new extension looking as if it had always been there*

using the materials to restore the core of the old castle, which was part medieval and part Georgian. It is built of rubble masonry, with slate freely used in the barrel-vaulted medieval cellars where the walls are 4 feet thick. Here there were earth floors, very damp, so the urgent priority was to put in a damp-proof course and dwarf walls on which floorboards were laid. Thus it is well ventilated.

The upper floors needed some considerable renovation to make them suitable for a young family to live in, but there was ample space for replanning, which meant that a new kitchen and a new drawing room could be built on, while the old kitchen was converted into a double garage, with two arched entrances, and floored in at ceiling height to make a playroom.

The clever part of this restoration is the way in which the material from the demolished wing has been put to such good use. Nothing has been wasted. For a start, the sale of the lead from the roof paid for the demolition. Slates were salvaged to be used in the new roof, cupboards were brought in for use in the castle store room, doors and skirting boards were used, if not in their entirety, for other purposes, and all flooring was saved for the restoration work. Window shutters were reused as cupboard doors, old bits of stair rail made good window frames, and even the broken-up plaster from the old house was utilized to make a cavity wall in a sandwich of plasterboard to provide a soundproof partition wall on a landing. This made an extra bathroom possible. Old pine facings were used in the new kitchen, where they now look thoroughly modern.

On the second floor, bedrooms have been brought up to date and good use has been made of all slopes by fitting in cupboards beneath them and installing Velux roof lights. A fire escape was contrived through a bedroom wall, out to the roof – a necessary precaution in such a remote spot, and one insisted upon by the authorities. All old beams and other woodwork were treated with insecticide, and recessed lights were fitted between beams to keep them as unobtrusive as possible. The whole place is centrally heated.

The Victorian wing had no fewer than seventeen chimney stacks, very tall and decorative, spirally fluted or panelled. These were dismantled very carefully and are now in use as ornamental garden containers and pots. They make a very attractive addition to the terrace and the lovely old walled garden. The old round tower has been preserved and restored as a feature, but some of the stonework had to be renewed. It was so well matched that it is quite undetectable.

There were many historic features in the original castle that were worth preserving, and this is but a brief, undetailed account of the rescue operation. Indeed, one could easily write a book on Ardmaddy Castle and its colourful history. But the point of this present-day restoration has been to make a home, to salvage something valuable from the past to bring into the present, and to hand on a heritage for the future, as beautiful as it is practical.

The restoration of this castle was a full-scale operation, with much of the work being done by the owners themselves, over a period of three years, and working to a very tight budget. Now, the place is manageable, and a source of great pleasure to all who live or visit there.

These two examples in Scotland – the smithy and the castle – illustrate my point: that no type of building need be wasted provided that it is structurally sound.

Obviously, the subject of stone, with all its permutations and variations, is a vast one, and it has only been possible here to touch on the fringe of it as it may affect the ordinary householder. If, however, there are any doubts about the quality of any stone, its suitability for a given area, or any problems about building construction and materials in relation to specific situations, the Building Research Establishment has an advisory service which is pleased to help, the address of which may be found in the Appendix.

5
Roofing

One of the charms of old houses is the variety of roofing materials they bear. The traditional coverings are thatch, clay tile and slate, and the men who put them up were highly skilled craftsmen in their own right. In many cases the evidence of their skill is still there for us to see.

In the past it is likely that local material would have been used on a house, and we still look for stone in the Cotswolds, in Horsham and other parts of Sussex, as well as locally in the north; slate in Scotland, Wales and the Lake District, away from the limestone belt; clay tiles in the south-east and the Midlands; and thatch wherever the raw material is to be found. It would have been considered out of keeping to introduce anything 'foreign' or not in regional style.

It is interesting to note that, with the exception of turf, the materials that were used for the first buildings ever erected in Britain are still being used. Thatch has been regaining interest because of its thermal properties. Clay tiles, introduced by the Romans, are still employed some sixteen centuries later. Slates also survive, in spite of the fact that many of the giant Welsh quarries have long since passed their Victorian heyday. From this, it may be argued that there is nothing to compare with these natural materials, even today.

A roof contributes so much to the look of a building that any covering that is out of place would ruin its overall appearance completely and destroy the authenticity of a period house quicker than anything else; so the golden rule for restoration and repair is to match the original as far as possible, using salvaged material if necessary.

There may, of course, be occasions when substitutes have to be used, either because the existing material has proved to be unsuitable, or for economic reasons. Where such a change is unavoidable, every effort should be made to achieve harmony with the old building. Externally, the shape of a roof gives a house its character and also gives a clue to its design, so it is important not to change any variation in the roof line, unless structural alterations demand otherwise. It would be a pity to change an interesting roof line into one of dull uniformity for no good reason.

The use of each of the roofing materials mentioned requires specialized techniques and each material plays its own unique part in the work of restoring an old roof. It is interesting to know something about them and the ways in which they can be renewed.

Thatch Anyone with a sense of beauty loves an old thatched cottage. It is part of the English countryside – 'unmitigated England', as Henry James called it – and fortunately it is something that we can still hold on to and cherish, for it is good to know that there is a real revival of interest in thatch. One used to hear the cry 'Thatching is a dying art!', but that is quite untrue, for today there are over eight hundred full-time thatchers in England and Wales, trained craftsmen, very often with a long waiting-list of clients.

Thatch, or 'thack' as it was originally called, has proved its worth

17　A strange mixture of thatched reed cottages at Mickleton, Gloucestershire. Old thatch to the left has some patched-in new thatch just showing at the edge to join a new ridge capping that continues and joins new thatch to the right. There are Cotswold stone roofing tiles on and around the dormer windows

over some thousands of years, though it was banned from London in the thirteenth century because of fire risk. It is still one of the glories of East Anglia, where the great wheatlands and reed beds of Broad and Fen provide the raw material. It is a first-rate roofing material – good to look at, durable, completely weatherproof, the perfect insulator and eminently practical in every way.

Not so many years ago thatch was looked down upon as the poor man's roofing material, so much so that the class-conscious Victorians were driven to tiling that part of the roof visible from the road and thatching the part that was hidden. Now, all that is changed and owners of thatched roofs prize them for their beauty as well as their durability, with the result that a great number of old roofs are being repaired or reconverted to their original state, a change of attitude that brings great benefit to the countryside.

It is a fairly costly business to put thatch where it never was before, because a roof has to have a properly constructed framework on to which thatch can be fastened, and the rafters are much more widely spaced than for a tiled roof. Nevertheless, a master thatcher is usually well able to carry out this conversion himself, overcoming problems of pitch while doing so or even building a new gable or constructing a dormer where necessary. He rarely resorts to the services of a carpenter, for his is an intensely individual craft, defying any kind of mechanization.

Conversely, it is equally expensive to convert a thatched roof to a tiled roof, because of the difference in pitch and the need for new rafters and purlins of sawn timber in place of the original rough supports. The moral seems to be that, unless expense is no object, the original material is better renewed than changed for some other.

It is an easy matter to rethatch or repair an old roof and it is always worthwhile if undertaken by an experienced craftsman. It never pays to employ a bodger who offers cheap work but who will prove to be infinitely more expensive in the long run.

There are three main kinds of thatching material in general use: Norfolk reed, combed wheat reed, sometimes called Devon reed, and long straw. Each of these requires a different technique for laying, varying according to traditional regional methods. Gable ends, dormers and roof ridges are also treated differently in each county and their shapes vary. It is almost impossible to find out the reason for these regional variations, though it would be very interesting to do so, but they all make for individuality and add a great deal of charm to the countryside.

The tools needed for thatching are simple, often made by the thatcher himself. They vary from county to county, together with the methods of work and the technical terms employed, which are quite impossible for the lay person to understand.

Put briefly, the techniques are as follows. The thatch is sewn to the roof battens with tarred cord threaded through a special stitching needle, or fixed to the common rafters with hazel rods and hooks. The rods and hooks are then covered by the topmost layer, until the last coat of thatch is pinned to the roof ridge. The thatcher works from the eaves upwards, spreading his material and raking it, or combing it, to an even surface – upwards for reed and downwards for straw.

With all these materials the ridge is treated in any number of different ways. It may be plain or flush, or it may be decorated with a pattern. Where the tough Norfolk reed is used, the ridge has to be made of sedge, a much more pliable material. As it matures sedge becomes a beautiful golden brown, and with its hazel cross-sparring and clean-shaped pattern it makes an attractive contrast both in tone and texture to the lighter gold of the Norfolk reed. Following an old custom, a thatcher will often fix his trademark on the end of a ridge, a symbol made of straw after the manner of a corn dolly, for all to see.

It may be considered an advantage in some cases to cover long straw thatch with wire netting, but it must be correctly fixed to avoid unsightliness. It must also be easily removable in an emergency.

There is another type of thatching, known as 'wood chip', which still exists on some very old cottages in parts of Sussex, though the method is dying out. There may be some people, however, who wish to replace it when necessary; I saw this being done in a remote village in Sussex. The thatch is made from lengths of wood, which used to be offcuts from hoops made of hazel or chestnut split down the centre, shaved, trimmed and tapered at both ends to make wedge-type bundles, like Norfolk reed. The thatcher has to make his own wood chips on the rare occasions he is called upon to do so, usually when an old building is being restored to its original form.

In this context, the restorer may be in for some surprises when he strips an old thatched roof. He may well discover a wattle foundation instead of laths, for this was the old English method. There is an interesting example of this in Quarley, Hampshire, where the original support for an old straw roof was a very rough wattling, held down to the roof timbers by a triangular piece of wood through which a peg was driven. The wattle was black and brittle with age and smoke, yet still holding together firmly when it was removed. It is interesting to recall that traces of the original smoke shaft were discovered, lined with wattle and daub thickly coated with the black barnacles of wood tar. This house, of medieval origin, had obviously passed through many phases in its long existence, and it has now been enlarged and converted into a delightful country home with a beautiful new thatched roof: a case where restoration paid handsome dividends.

Some people protest that thatching is too expensive for them to reinstate, but this is not so when one considers its advantages. It is completely waterproof – the rain just slides off the reeds or straw and no gutters are needed. It is cool in summer and warm in winter and is extremely durable. If it is sheltered from prevailing winds and is not under tall trees where drippings will encourage moss to grow, a Norfolk reed thatch can last seventy years or more, combed wheat reed about forty years and long straw from twenty to thirty years. This is a modest estimate, for there have been cases where a much longer life has been proved. In the final analysis its length of life depends upon a number of factors – the quality of the material, weather conditions and, most important of all, the skill of the thatcher.

When a roof has been newly thatched, an arrangement can be made with the thatcher to inspect it every two or three years, and in this way any defects can be corrected without delay.

It is not difficult to contact a suitable thatcher in a given area, thanks to such bodies as CoSIRA and the Crafts Council, who are always pleased to put inquirers in touch with local craftsmen.

Shingles, or wooden tiles On old cottages, where the roof was previously thatched and the rafters are not strong enough to take heavy tiles, shingles can be the ideal compromise. In medieval times they were made of oak, cut by hand in such a way that the grain of the wood served as tiny spouts for the water. The carpenters overlapped them in a neat pattern on the steeply pointed roofs, so that no snow could drift in between them and no rain could penetrate. They were never as popular as thatch and a sharp rise in the cost of timber between the fifteenth and sixteenth centuries made them uneconomic, but their durability was unquestionable and some fifteenth-century oak shingles can still be found in places in remarkably good condition, mellowed and weathered to a deep, silvery grey. Obviously they cannot be renewed nowadays, but Canadian cedar tiles are a very good replacement and are easily obtained. When new they are usually sprayed with a wood preservative to prevent woodworm, and in time they weather to a soft, silvery grey so that they blend in with any setting. They have an average life of fifty years and cost very little more than tiles. Against that, the roof rafters do not need to be strengthened as for tiles, so a comparison of costs may well decide in their favour. Another choice is that of Western red cedar shakes, which are similar to shingles but thicker than the modern ones, tapering from $1\frac{1}{2}$ inches to $\frac{1}{2}$ inch in thickness. They are not much used in Britain but very popular in North America. They are laid on the roof so that there are at least three thicknesses of timber at any given point, and have a longer life than shingles. The main drawbacks of wooden tiles are the risk of fire, the slightly higher insurance premium demanded as a result and, in some places, restrictions imposed by local by-laws.

Clay tiles   A weather-stained, many-tinted tiled roof on an old house is a feature to be preserved and certainly not to be discarded lightly. Possibly there will be a gentle irregularity about it which indicates that the tiles are hand-made and may even be bedded down on moss or hay as they were in the old days, to keep the snow from driving underneath. Some of the undulations may be due to the sagging or warping of rafters or laths, but within reasonable limits this does not matter and, indeed, adds to the visual appeal.

Tiles varied in size according to the locality and this is seen to good effect in the peg tiles of the Kent and Sussex Weald and in the rippling Dutch pantiles brought to the eastern counties by Protestant refugees from the Low Countries in the eighteenth century. Apart from the aesthetic qualities of these hand-made tiles they are also immensely practical and long-lasting, as any old building's records will confirm.

18   *Old Dutch pantiles in need of restoration. They have been badly patched with cement*

19 *Old Kentish peg tiled roof, with the pegs still clearly in evidence*

This makes it unlikely that all the tiles on an old roof will need renewing at the same time. Even where, for other reasons, the roof has to be stripped, many of the old clay tiles will be reusable if care is taken when they are being dismantled.

Formerly they were hung on riven oak battens and attached by means of oak pegs driven through the holes and hooked over the battens. Pantiles were 'torched', or pointed, on the underside with lime mortar. When an old building is being demolished one often comes across tiles or stone slates with the wooden pegs still in them, and this may well be the time to buy some back from the builder's yard for replacement purposes.

It is usually the battens that need replacing first and in these days heavy-gauge deal is used instead of oak. It may be found that iron fixing nails were used on oak and that these have been eaten away by the tannic acid always present in oak. This means that any nails used in fixing battens to oak timbers should be either made of copper or heavily galvanized.

It may, incidentally, still be possible to use the oak pegs, depending on their condition, but towards the end of the last century it became general practice to make tiles with a small projecting clay hook on the underside, known as a nib. Now, practically all tiles are nibbed in the making, but they will also be nailed in every third or fifth course, according to the quality of the work.

It is possible to get broken or damaged tiles copied by a tiler, for the making of sand-faced tiles by hand is by no means extinct. To get first-hand information I visited one of the few remaining family firms who specialize in this work, and followed the process of making clay tiles from the moment of digging the clay from the pit to their emergence from the kiln, ready for use. There is an amazing variety to be matched in restoration work. Apart from plain roofing tiles and Roman-type interlocking tiles (pantiles) there are also Granny Bonnet Hips, which are in demand where there is a preservation order on a building. The old Granny Bonnet hip tiles, bedded in mortar and each having a decided 'lift', add great charm to a roof, and so can the saddle-back ridge tiles on the angles of hipped roofs.

Sometimes the ridge tiles were designed to come up almost to a point; sometimes they took the form of half-round or hog-back tiles of generous size. There are also some quite elaborate crest tiles on some houses – probably originally made in terra cotta. Many quite ordinary Victorian houses still have some remarkable crests and finials.

All of these need different techniques for moulding and making, some taking a tighter gauge of clay than others. Beside the tile maker is a pile of fine moulding sand, and both the mould and the unfired clay are sprinkled with sand to produce a pleasing texture. Where old tiles have to be matched for restoration purposes some manganese powder is added to the sand in sufficient quantity to determine the colour and, as one can imagine, it takes considerable expertise to judge the right amount, as it does to assess the exact time for firing. In all these things no modern technology can take the place of a man's shrewd, experienced judgement.

This particular firm also makes hanging tiles for walls, which are slightly thinner than those used for roofs and made in a surprising variety of patterns, some having half-round ends, some with a flange at each side or with some other slight difference that marks them out for attention, giving a fish-scaled effect.

The colours of hand-made tiles vary from soft brown to old mellowed red, and they have an attractive textured, weathered look as soon as they come out of the kiln. In fact, it is this look and texture that distinguishes them from the machine-made variety which, by comparison, look flat and lifeless.

Structurally, hand-made tiles are better for the roof, too. They do not lie so flat, their gently cambered surface conforming more easily with the slight irregularities of an old timber roof, and in this way they allow the air to get to the timbers so that they can 'breathe'. Another attraction is that they tend to encourage the growth of lichens and

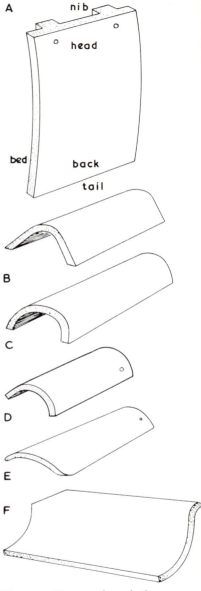

Fig. 14 *Types of roof tile.*
A. *Plain tile B. Hogs back ridge
C. Half-round ridge D. Cone
hip E. Bonnet hip F. Pantile*

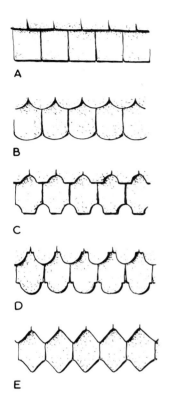

Fig. 15 *Hanging tiles. A. Plain hanging tile B. The Beaver C. Fish tail   D. The Butt E. Arrowhead*

mosses, which do no harm at all and add to the interest and charm of an old roof.

They are not unduly expensive compared with the machine-made product, which are mostly concrete these days, and certainly when new hand-made tiles are used in conjunction with salvaged original tiles, the cost is very favourable.

There are, of course, some very good concrete tiles on the market today, and it is possible to get them in a weathered, antique colour, so that they do not look too conspicuous on an old building. It is advisable to go to an accredited roofing advice centre before making a decision.

Slates   Most people think of roofing slates as the ordinary thin Welsh ones that are seen in such profusion in most big cities. They were the nineteenth-century's most popular roofing material, brought about by the Industrial Revolution and the large-scale mechanical production of machine-split slates when easier transport became available. Before that time, English slates were smaller and rougher in texture, bearing some resemblance to limestone.

To fulfil its purpose true slate must be hard and fissile, varying in colour from grey and green to blue or black, the quality and texture depending to a large extent on the locality from which it comes. Cornish and Devon slates are beautifully textured. Those from Bangor in North Wales are a dull blue-purple colour; Irish slates are somewhat tougher and heavier; and English slates from Westmorland, Lancashire and Cornwall are thick, with a rough surface and jagged edges, a beautiful grey-green colour. They all have picturesque trade names, too, which add to their attraction – Ladies, Viscountesses, Countesses, Duchesses, Princesses and Queens, according to their size. There are also 'doubles'.

All slates are laid on a roof of fairly low pitch, in courses, with the longest next to the eaves and the shortest at the ridge. There is a practical advantage in this, because as the bigger slates are at the lower part of the roof over which most of the rain water passes, there are fewer nail holes for it to penetrate.

The ridges of these slate roofs were originally formed by random lengths of freestone chiselled into shape and bedded on with lime mortar, and it may still be possible to see some of these about the country now, though they have long since been superseded by ridge tiles of Staffordshire clay in standard lengths.

In some cases, slates are preferable to tiles, especially in exposed situations, because they are less absorbent and are laid on a roof of lower pitch; but as they are conductors of heat, they make the upper rooms cold in winter and hot in summer.

Original hand-made slates, with their slight irregularity, look infinitely better than machine-split slates on an old house, the old style of slate seeming to complement the old style of building. There are still some quarries working where it is possible to replace old slates, in their original form, and it is well worth making inquiries and getting estimates. The National Federation of Roofing Contractors is pleased to advise householders.

Stone slates   In this context, the word 'slates' is a misnomer. However, it has crept into common usage and we must continue with it, to avoid confusion.

Since carefully selected stone was reckoned to last at least two hundred years, there must be many surviving stone roofs around the countryside, for the material is plentiful in parts of the north of England and in those regions covered by the great limestone belt, from Dorset to east Yorkshire, including Hereford and Worcester and the Welsh border counties. Horsham, and elsewhere in Sussex, is also noted for its stone; indeed, Horsham stone is one of the finest roofing materials available, practically indestructible. I have seen some splendid examples of quite ancient roofs both in Horsham and in Wales, in excellent condition. The colour and texture of the old stone seem to merge in with the landscape as few other materials can, and when fixed on hand-riven timber the slates have a gentle, wavy irregularity that is very pleasing to the eye. Often a dappling of green and gold lichen adds to their venerable appearance. An old stone roof on an old stone house is truly beautiful.

In the old days the stone, like slate, had to be naturally fissile so that a skilled man could cleave it along the fissure and trim each piece with a hammer. Then each slate was holed near its head so that it could be fixed on to the roof lath, either with oak pegs or iron nails, a practice which present-day craftsmen condemn as unsatisfactory, preferring to use copper nails.

The slates are usually about 1 inch thick, laid in diminishing courses, growing gradually smaller from eaves to ridge; that is, the heaviest stones are laid just above the eaves, so that the walls take the weight of them, the next in weight are laid above them, overlapping the ones beneath, and so on, until the ridge is reached. The ridge is normally formed out of solid sawn or split stone, and the valleys (the roof intersections) are usually of triangular slabs, producing a soft curve which is one of the particular charms of this roofing material.

In the Cotswolds there seemed to be no attempt made to produce stones of uniform size, and each stone was chosen for its suitability in a given position. The result is a delightful medley of beautiful roofs, artistically satisfying, yet the product of great practical skill.

The old-time Cotswold slaters also used a quaint language of their own to describe the kind of slate they were using, its size and weight. There were, for example, Bachelors, Movedays, Rogue-why-winkest-Thou, Jenny-why-gettest-Thou, Short Backs, Long Backs, Shorts Save One, and many others, all equally imaginative. It is doubtful if one would ever hear this kind of language spoken now, but the old stone slates to which it referred remain.

In medieval days the stone slates were bedded on moss, as were clay tiles, with the lowest layers 'torched', or pointed, on the underside to keep the roof watertight. Because they were not entirely flat, the roof also had to be of a moderately steep pitch to keep the rain from driving in. The stones are weighty, and need a strong supporting framework to take them. It is usually this wooden framework which is the first part of the roof structure to need attention, and it is very important that this should be kept in good order.

Sometimes the stones shift a little and need some additional mortar to keep them in place. Where this is necessary it should be kept well back and unseen – a roof excessively flushed up with mortar loses its aesthetic appeal. Alternatively, heavy stones may need to be wired to the rafters with copper wire to prevent their weight causing any movement.

A stone slate roof is highly practical on any house in an exposed place. Being non-conductors of heat, the stones keep a house cool in summer and warm in winter, and are worth preserving wherever possible.

When there is insufficient of the original roofing material to be found, be it tiles, slate or stone, it is a good idea to use any salvaged material on the parts of the roof that will show, reserving new for the parts that are hidden. In this way the appearance of a house will be preserved.

When using salvaged tiles, great care should be taken not to mix the patterns, bearing in mind that each variety of tile has a different 'lay'. Unless they are all of one kind, rain will assuredly find a way through the odd crevices.

Where new tiles have to be used in conjunction with old, with no means of separating them, the hard, uninteresting appearance of the machine-made tile can sometimes be avoided by the discreet mixing of old tiles with new, for they soon begin to tone down together and give additional texture and colour to the building. Any new slates should be set in the same way as the original ones. If new tiles are used alone, it is a good idea to get a variety of colours, to avoid uniformity.

Tiling should be started from the bottom and worked upwards, from left to right. The nibs should be firmly fixed over the laths they rest on, so that the lay is even, with the gauge not less than 4 inches in order to ensure that rain does not enter through the joints.

In some cases, it may be a comparatively simple job for a handyman to repair his own roof, to replace a tile or fix a slipping slate which could be a potential danger to the public, but he should at the same time look for the cause of the defect. It may mean that nails are rusting or that roof timbers are beginning to rot. Rain penetrating through loose tiles or slates can do a great deal of damage over a period of time, not only to the timbers but to internal decorations.

Fig. 16   *Common roofing terms*

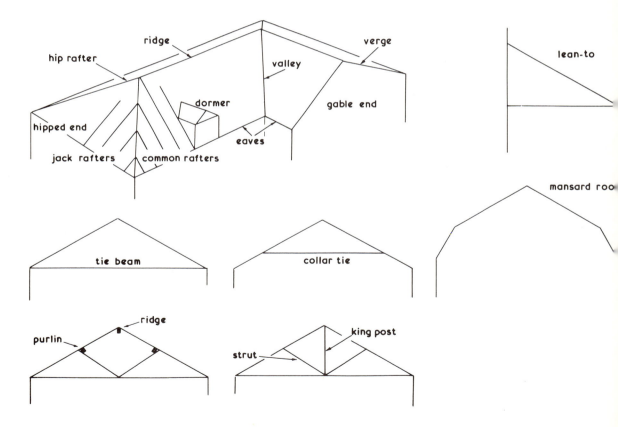

The roof timbers should be carefully checked to make sure that the rafters are sound. They may need bracing or packing up so that the roof tiles will lie correctly. This is a small fault that can lead to a lot of trouble.

For complete weatherproofing, tiles should be pointed underneath or given a lining, such as bitumen-filled felt, which is very strong. The felt is fixed above the rafters and below the battens on which the tiles are laid, carried well into the gutters and secured with clout nails.

Other points to be checked on an old roof are the valleys, which may be lined with lead. If this is corroded, it allows water to penetrate behind a slate or tile. Chimney stacks should also be examined for signs of the mortar crumbling between the brickwork or the stonework. They may need repointing or even rebuilding to make them quite safe. Incidentally, a slight leaning inwards towards the roof on an old cottage need not be alarming. The old-time builders

Fig. 17 *Lead roofing. Shown here compressed – the distance between steps or 'drips' could be up to 30 inches. At the top there is flashing into brickwork. The gutter fits similarly into the parapet wall. At all joints there is ample overlap to prevent water reaching underneath, and on the rolls the 'overcloak' goes far enough to make the joint waterproof*

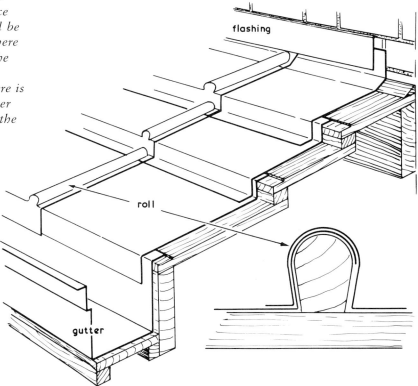

often built chimney stacks this way deliberately, so that if they were in danger from high winds they would fall on to the roof rather than on to the ground, and possibly on the heads of passers-by.

Having assessed the general state of the roof and taken all faults into account, it may be considered more satisfactory in the long run to renew the entire roof rather than patch it, with the possibility of recurring expense in the future for further repairs. Material and methods used for reroofing an old building will depend upon the type and condition of the original structure as well as on the intended future life of the building. The choice of standard, therefore, is highly important, and when seeking estimates the householder should avoid cheapjack or 'cowboy' firms, however inviting their offers may appear. There is a grave risk of shoddy workmanship with no redress for the customer should trouble arise from it. Your house is too valuable an asset to risk in this way. There are many approved roofing contractors available who will guarantee their workmanship for at least ten years, and these are the recommended ones to use. There are also advice centres in various parts of the country where the householder can get expert advice on any roofing problem.

In general, it is not advisable to use any kind of surface roof coating which is offered as a cheap method of sealing the existing roof material. In practice these coatings may in time cause condensation and subsequently crack with any natural movement of the roof sub-structure. Under the Code of Practice for Slating and Tiling this method is not recommended either for internal or external application.

There is for the do-it-yourself owner a very useful Roof and Guttering Repair Kit which has recently come on to the market. It is in effect a first-aid box for the home, enabling the householder to deal with minor repairs and emergency waterproofing immediately. These problems, if not attended to quickly, can cause an enormous amount of expensive damage, and this kit must be a welcome item in any household, especially those in remote areas where immediate help is not easily obtained. It is made by BP Aquaseal.

6
Fireplaces and Chimneys

Few parts of a period house have suffered more at the hands of would-be restorers than its fireplaces. Successive generations have wrecked them, putting in their place something they imagined to be modern and improved at the time, and in doing so they have taken away the essential character of a room. What more charming than an inglenook in a cottage, or the classic beauty of an Adam-design fireplace in a Georgian house? Each period had its unique architectural features and a fireplace is surely the most distinctive, worthy of restoration or reinstatement.

In fact, no full-scale restoration could possibly be authentic without the fireplaces that were in use at the period. A room would very often be designed around its fireplace, where the family assembled, and the same applied in cottage or castle. It was literally the 'family circle'.

The installation of a fireplace where none previously existed (as in the conversion of an old barn, coach house or similar building) is a comparatively simple matter, though the work may need approval under the building regulations.

A new fireplace for an old building should be chosen very carefully, taking into account the proportions of the room, its period and its general atmosphere. There are many ready-made fireplaces on the market today, to suit all situations. The manufacturers are always presenting us with new designs, some of them good, others totally unsuitable for an old building. Do not be misled by spurious talk about 'bringing a room to life'; some of the designs would kill it, though they might look very effective in an ultra-modern setting. The restorer must be very discriminating in this respect.

Some modern reproduction fireplaces are excellent, but the detail may not relate to the period or the architectural style of the room for which it is wanted. It is worth delving into some old pattern books to check these finer points, also to make sure of getting a grate to match the fireplace. This is all highly important, for it is a feature you hope to live with for many years to come, the focal point to which your eye will be drawn as soon as you enter the room. If it is out of tune, aesthetically speaking, it will be a source of irritation rather than pleasure and the purist in you will rebel. On the practical side, you may be spending a good deal of money on this one feature so it is worth getting it right from all standpoints.

Restoring to the original is not quite as easy as a straightforward conversion or beginning from scratch, so to speak. It all depends on the form of the original, whether it was an inglenook, a Georgian dog grate with carved mantelshelf, or a Victorian marble chimneypiece with a small high grate. The period of the house will decide what was there when it was built, even if something else has since been superimposed on it; but whatever the original may have been, correctly restored it will give the room its period character to which every other feature will be related.

The small period cottage seems to have been the victim of more so-called 'improvements' than most, and many a fine original inglenook has been ruthlessly buried behind, first, a Victorian grate, then an 'all-night burner' or modern tiled grate, without taste or character.

Sometimes it is possible to find evidence of lost fireplaces by taking a look at the outside of the house and tracing chimneys to their appropriate fireplaces inside. Some may have been blocked up, or hidden in some way, and a wall that sounds hollow when tapped may give a clue as to their whereabouts; but where there are back-to-back fireplaces and an axial chimney stack, the size of the chimney breast and the volume lost between the two rooms give a clue to the original structure.

Excavation should proceed with great caution so as not to endanger the structure of the old fireplace in the process of removing the new. The outline of timber or stone lintels can sometimes be traced to give an idea of the size of the original fireplace opening and a gentle probe through the plaster about 4 to 5 feet from the floor may determine if one is still in place. If the lintel is still there it may need temporary support while the existing grate is being taken out, to avoid collapse. At the same time great care should be taken not to damage any original features such as stone mouldings, carvings, old tiles and so on. They may be valuable. Also, there may be evidence of some old fireplace furniture, like a chimney crane, a bar for pothangers and for the suspension of a spit or a stock pot, or cast-iron firebacks. The latter were used to protect the brickwork at the back of the open fireplace from the fierce heat of the flames, and they also helped to throw the heat into the room. They made a useful and picturesque addition to the hearth. None of these furnishings should be removed unless it is absolutely necessary.

Most exciting of all may be the discovery of an old cloam oven, a very old feature that was probably in existence in Tudor times. Built at the right-hand side of the open hearth at shoulder level, it had a stone floor and dome-shaped roof. When it was used for baking, a wood fire was laid on the floor to heat it and as soon as a high enough temperature had been reached the burning embers were scooped out and bread or oat cakes were baked in the oven on a bakestone, or 'backstone'. The entrance to the oven was sealed with a large stone or stones. Sometimes the oven was used to warm a flat stone for use as a bed warmer, so its uses were by no means restricted.

Ovens of this kind are commonplace in the Scottish border country and in some Welsh and Cornish houses even today, but they are invariably fitted with iron doors. The cloam ovens are much earlier, though it is difficult to discover just how far back they go. One came to light a short time ago during the restoration of a Welsh house near Wrexham and was reckoned to be between three and four hundred years old and part of what had once been a large inglenook.

I have seen bread ovens still in use in remote rural areas and they bake excellent bread; it is obviously well worthwhile to put them in good order, ready for use.

Where a chimney stack was built as a projection, brick and clay ovens were often built into the hearths, seen from the outside as round or rectangular protuberances, and those extending beyond the outer wall face were provided with their own roof. The modern housewife may not want such a large bread oven but there are other uses for it. In one cottage I saw an oven that had been opened up and converted into a small semi-circular room that was used specially for telephoning. It housed a table for the telephone, a chair, a rack for directories, some books and other small items. It disposed of necessary clutter very neatly besides being an ingenious use of space.

Although it is a major operation to excavate a fireplace that may be up to 6 feet across and 3 feet deep, it can be immensely rewarding. This was the case in a cottage in Titchfield, Hampshire, where a young couple were restoring two cottages, each two hundred years old, making them into one. They realized there was some essential feature missing in their living room. The wall around the modern tiled fireplace (which they disliked) sounded hollow when tapped, so they took a chance and pulled it out, together with its matchboard surround, removing at the same time several layers of Victorian wallpapers. Their first find was a Victorian grate, of no great charm. They excavated still further and were rewarded when the original inglenook fireplace appeared with a thick oak mantel beam intact.

Taking care to support the heavy beam on stout upright posts, they began work on the chimney, removing four sacks of soot and several hundredweights of bricks and rubble in the process. They spent some days working actually up the chimney – a capacious one – sweeping it by hand, removing and replacing any crumbling bricks and reversing others. During this time they found some old coins – one a George III dated 1790, which was well after the cottage was built – and a perfectly preserved mummified mouse! They also found a cavity, not big enough for a priest's hole but it could well have been a cache. The whole of the chimney was repointed and a trap door was fitted high up in it, controlled from the bottom of the fireplace so that it can be closed when no fire is burning. Next, they concreted the floor and fitted a brick kerb; then they chipped a channel in the floor to the outside of the house and laid pipes to bring in air, with the result that a log fire now burns splendidly and seldom goes out in winter. The old oak beam was given a hood of copper-clad steel beneath it, to channel the smoke upwards and take the fumes from the room. In the summer this huge, brick-lined inglenook is converted into an indoor garden, illuminated by a strip light concealed behind the beam. Few people guess that the beautiful 'garden' is actually contained in an old sink, picked up from an old junk shop and camouflaged with some pieces of Bath stone, collected at odd times in the car.

The restoration of this venerable inglenook at once gave the room that air of security and comfort which rightly belongs to an old English cottage.

Sometimes the restoration of these Tudor 'hole-in-the-wall' fireplaces yields many more exciting finds than a mummified mouse. It is not uncommon to find a 'luck token' in the form of old shoes, gloves, coins or other small items, which were often deposited at a time of some major domestic event or improvement. They help to date a house, or at least part of it. At Eyhorne Manor, Hollingbourne, Kent, a child's shoe and a human bone were found buried in the chimney. They were probably put there in the first place to encourage fertility. In some of the cruck houses in the Yorkshire Dales there would be a 'witch post' supporting the cross beam of the fireplace, with some strange carvings on it, the origins of which are shrouded in mystery. Belief in magic was widespread for centuries and it was said that witches were powerless to enter or wreak harm to a room guarded by a witch post. Odd finds like this give a fascinating glimpse into the strange superstitions and folklore surrounding the fireplace, and they certainly whet the appetite for pursuing the subject further.

Simpler problems were encountered at Court Lees Cottage (des-

20   *The restored inglenook at Court Lees Cottage. The mantel beam is a railway sleeper*

cribed in Chapter 2) where there was a fireplace in one gable end wall, its flue linking up with a small fireplace in the bedroom immediately above. This fireplace, in the living room, should have been the dominating feature, the centre of attraction. Instead, it was a nondescript solid-fuel room heater, surrounded by pine panelling in a very rough state. The new owners decided to investigate, and levering out the panelling with a crow-bar they came to an iron range. They removed this, very carefully so as not to damage the walls more than necessary, and the original brick-lined inglenook came to light, very wide and deep – but the old bricks had all been painted bright red. The mantel beam turned out to be an iron girder, faced with a thin piece of timber, shoddily put up. The ideal would have been to replace this with an oak beam, but this was not possible without causing considerable damage, so an excellent alternative was found in the shape of a railway sleeper which was well scrubbed, sanded and treated with insecticide before being bolted to the girder. Brick jambs were built out at each side of the wall to take the weight, which means that the beam stands a few inches proud of the wall, giving a useful shelf on which to place a clock and some ornaments. Given a final polish, the old sleeper looks almost as good as oak and is just as serviceable.

The bricks lining the cavity were in very poor condition, which was probably why they had been painted over in the first place. It was decided to conceal them behind plaster, painted white, which serves to radiate the heat as well as the light. The exception was the back wall, behind the fire, where new local bricks were used as a backing, protected from the flames by a splendid cast-iron fireback of traditional design. Some salvaged square red tiles, of slightly rough texture, were found for the hearth, set in around an iron plate beneath the fire basket. Their warm, mellow look adds to the general feeling of comfort. The simplest style of iron fire basket was chosen, to take large logs, and it has a pair of dogs and an iron hood which tapers up into the flue, all made to measure by a local blacksmith, who also fitted an iron plate and register door above. A neat sliding ventilator was fitted into the hearth, but this was hardly necessary for the fire burns brightly at all times and there has never been any trouble with the flue. This was another excavation that was well worthwhile, transforming the entire atmosphere of the cottage to one of great charm and character.

In some old farmhouses the recessed fireplace was more like a self-contained kitchen, occupying practically the whole of one wall. It often had seats built within it, a whole range of cooking utensils stored there, and a bread oven in one wall as well as a salt box in a recess in the wall near the hearth, where salt could be kept dry. The chimney, too, had its uses. Bacon was placed in a special smoke chamber leading off the flue, where it was cured and stored. It was an ingenious use of space and heat, and in at least one house I found the old smoke chamber restored to its original use. I doubt if anyone has better-tasting bacon!

Present-day restorers are finding other imaginative uses for these homely fireplaces and their appurtenances. In one cottage a vast inglenook was excavated in the room destined to be a garage and the owners, determined to use all space to the maximum, turned this area into a self-contained laundry. After they had removed all bricks and rubble from the fireplace cavity, they repaired the walls and concreted and tiled the floor. Walls and ceiling were then panelled with formica, and a fluorescent strip light and two power points were fitted. A stainless steel sink unit with hot and cold water (all pipes lagged), a washing machine and a spin dryer make this a very useful utility room and save space in the cottage kitchen. An outlet hose to the top of the chimney and an extractor fan in the ceiling discharge general damp air (via hose joining hose), and finally the chimney top was panelled over (except for the hose outlet) to keep out rain. It is the most ingenious use I have yet encountered for a disused fireplace and while, strictly speaking, it cannot be classed as restoration, it is a good idea in a utilitarian place like a garage and it keeps the cottage itself from being invaded by too many modern devices. But those who are thinking of copying would be well advised to study local building regulations in advance.

Although the inglenook seems to catch the fancy of the restorer more than most, and it is seen in many guises, the general design of fireplaces represents some facets of every period.

From the primitive central hearth we progressed towards the wall fireplace in stone during Tudor times. Typical of this period is the stone frame with a four-centred arch over it, the jambs chamfered and stopped high up with a decorative feature such as a Tudor rose or a shield carved in the spandrels and lined with stone or herringbone-patterned brickwork. This was followed by the classical style, with a more lavish use of ornamentation, and in the homes of the wealthy the fireplace became the central feature of applied art in all important rooms. The royal coat of arms took pride of place in all decorations, with shields or floral emblems carved in stone, wood or brick as an overmantel.

It was not until much later, in the latter half of the seventeenth century, that the architect came on the scene and fireplace designs were incorporated into his plans and were seen as an essential part of the interior design of a room. Regular classical forms took the place of some of the more extravagant designs for chimneypieces that had gone before, and Inigo Jones introduced a type of marble mantel which was followed throughout the eighteenth century. Then came the Georgian age and the Adam style which has been imitated ever since, sometimes indiscriminately. The Victorian period, on the whole, abandoned all ideas of Georgian harmony and gave us heavy marble, wood or cast-iron fireplaces. But whatever type of fireplace the restorer may encounter, if it is original it will be expressive of its age and is therefore worthy of preservation.

The Gothic stonemasons' carving, the Elizabethan wall paintings, the marble sculptures and woodcarvings were all done by individual craftsmen using beautiful, natural materials, and they should be restored by present-day craftsmen who are trained in the appropriate skills.

Stonemasons are very well equipped to deal with stone carvings and they also work in marble. Architectural woodcarvers are prepared to restore carved wood chimneypieces, some of which were by unknown eighteenth-century craftsmen. These fireplaces are mostly in pine, with enrichments carved in lime, pinned and glued to the main part after the manner of Grinling Gibbon, that greatest of all woodcarvers. These enrichments could be anything from the formal flute and dart frieze to the most elaborate fantasies of fruit, flowers and scrolls. Not surprisingly such carvings have been subject to a good deal of damage over the years, but they are still capable of being restored by the expert in a way which makes it impossible to distinguish the old from the new. It is also possible to buy reproduction chimneypieces, but they should be bought from a craftsman with a knowledge of the period so that you can be sure that they are faithful copies of the original.

There are some craftsmen who specialise in the reclamation and restoration of Victorian fireplaces, kitchen stoves and ranges as well as all kinds of Victorian metalwork and castings. They offer general

21   *A restored Georgian fireplace, carved and ornamented after the manner of Grinling Gibbon*

shotblasting and polishing services, which literally give new life to many an old rusting article.

Restoration of the fireplace includes the grate, and this is a most important part of the whole. When coal began to take the place of wood there were various kinds of grate made to take it and keep it within safe limits in the hearth. They were made to complement the design of the fireplace and in any kind of restoration it is essential that the grate is of the correct style and period, otherwise the one will destroy the effect of the other.

Most of the early fireplaces had big fire baskets, designed to take logs, and these are easily restored, or copied, by a blacksmith, who will make an individual grate to fit the opening.

Later, in the Georgian era – from about 1714 to 1830 – some of the most beautiful dog grates ever seen were designed, the fronts generally of bright steel, with some parts of brass. In this respect we owe a great deal to the Carron Company, those great Scottish ironfounders who nurtured the genius of John Adam and the Haworth brothers. From delicate, intricate Adam designs, the Carron men made castings fretted and woven like black lace, with sweep and line, balance and proportion to enhance their beauty. The influence of these designers can be seen in several rare castings of early date for panels, fire grates, chimneypieces, balconies, balustrades, and so on. Anyone wishing to restore or reinstate a fireplace of this period would do well to visit the Victoria & Albert Museum, Kensington, which houses some of the best of this work; but there is also a good deal to be seen in many eighteenth-century houses. Where any Georgian architecture is preserved there is bound to be some of this beautiful work in evidence.

In Victorian times the most distinctive design was the hob grate, which came into use during the last half of the eighteenth century. The fronts were in cast iron, the bars, bowed or rounded, in wrought iron. The side panels were ornamented with great delicacy, often in the formal style of the Adam brothers. There were three types of hob grate: the double semi-circle, the double ogee and those with rectangular cheeks. They were placed in a square recess surrounded by a frame of stone or marble. The recess above the hob had a plastered back slanting up the chimney, and the sides were either plastered or lined with plates of fluted iron or Dutch tiles. There was no register door, but the short distance between the fire bars and the lintel prevented too much smoking. Many early Victorian houses have these distinctive grates, often set within the context of a heavy marble mantelshelf with wide jambs set with coloured marbles in the

22 *A late eighteenth-century double-ogee hob grate in a house at Brighton. The Victorian tiled hearth is intact (By courtesy of A. J. Da Vall)*

panels (Plate 22). It is sad to think of how many of these imposing fireplaces have been ripped out, together with their priceless tiles and other items that went with that particular period of fireplace architecture.

So far as the ironwork is concerned, the best craftsman to approach to restore it is the small ironfounder: choose one who specializes in good decorative domestic ironwork. He will recast panels to the original design, make oven doors and any other parts that are missing. As in other crafts, if no original item is available as a pattern, he will make one from a drawing or a photograph, using plaster of Paris, wood, plasticine or any other suitable material for a model. He can reproduce almost any design in this way; it is not an unusual thing, for example, for a client to order a fireback with his family crest on it, or some other personal insignia. It was common practice to do this in the Middle Ages when the fireback often recorded family happenings as well as important current events.

The same applies to firedogs, those 'ancient twin servitors of the hearth', so necessary to support the logs in an open fireplace. They range from the simple, functional design, expressive of the craftsman's own ideas rather than any set pattern, to the more elaborate styles of the seventeenth century. They are an imposing part of the fireplace and can give it great dignity. There are also the fire irons, by which we mean shovel, tongs, poker, log fork, etc., implements which came into more general use in the eighteenth century as coal supplanted all other types of fuel. They were practical tools but, being made by craftsmen, were usually decorative and, in the average home, made of steel or brass. Fenders were used for coal-burning grates, and they, too, were made as ornamental as possible, often matching the apron of the grate. Steel or brass club fenders were used in Victorian times and were very practical, as they are today, in the right setting.

Most of this fireplace furniture can be reproduced today, and it is worthwhile searching for the authentic item to complete a period fireplace.

Installing a new fireplace Where a fireplace is still in position, the fireback and firebricks should be examined, and if they are not in good condition they should be replaced. But it may be that an original fireplace has been torn out or ruined in some way by a previous owner so that it is beyond restoration and the only remedy is the complete installation of a new fireplace. This need not be as daunting as it sounds. The do-it-yourself enthusiast has in fact a tremendous choice of materials and designs nowadays. There are many firms specializing in supplying working drawings of fireplaces and replicas of classical patterns. It is possible, for instance, to buy a fireplace kit of reconstructed stone, with a numbered stone-by-stone diagram to follow.

No great technical expertise is needed to design an individual fireplace surround to restore a room to its original character. It is a matter of commonsense to make sure that the materials chosen for use near the fire are incombustible. Some of the more obvious ones are polished marble, natural stone – polished, sawn or riven – brick, slate in various colours, ceramic fireplace tiles and metal tiles, smooth or textured.

There is no practical limit to the height of a fireplace, but there are other important dimensions to be noted, such as the overall width of the wall and the width and projection of the chimney breast, as well as the position of windows. Adequate hearth projection and/or a kerb is necessary because of the possible danger from falling embers. The minimum distance for the use of combustible materials in front of an open fire or openable room heater is 12 inches, and 9 inches in any other case. A distance of 6 inches is required at the sides and back. The back distance generally depends on the thickness of the wall behind. It is worth noting that the hearth and the construction of the walling above the level of the hearth length should comply with the relevant building regulations. A copy of these can be bought from HM Stationery Office, or can be consulted at a local library.

Smoke control Generally speaking, once an original fireplace is restored the problem of smoke control arises. In the old days people had enormous fires with plenty of draught to keep them going. Now that we no longer want, or can afford, these huge fires, it is better to confine the fire to an inner fireplace and channel the draught by a hood tapering up into the flue; the success of any open fire depends, however, upon the construction of the flues as well as the chimney. In practice, a flue is a rectangular shaft enclosed within a chimney stack which may also include flues from more than one fireplace. For the efficient operation of the fire it is essential to have a smooth, funnel-shaped 'gather' that begins at the top of the opening and gradually tapers into the chimney proper. The truth is that any chimney will smoke under certain conditions: when the top is surrounded by air condensed by pressure, while the air below is in its normal state. This happens when a chimney stands near an object higher than itself. A strong gust of wind may strike the object without touching the chimney itself and by pressure condense the air below it, driving it down the mouth of the chimney and in any other direction where no resistance is offered. This is quite well understood today and the problem is usually dealt with by fitting a type of cowl on the chimney pot to meet the particular situation.

Old chimney stacks need careful inspection to eliminate the danger of fire from faulty flues. The old stacks were built with wide bases to accommodate the huge fireplaces and tapered like a pyramid as they reached the roof, but when later generations added fireplaces and new flues they often cut away part of the original structure without regard to future safety. The part of the stack that is hidden from sight between the bedroom ceilings and the roof is most likely to be out of repair and should be examined carefully. While repairing a stack it should also, if necessary, be restored to the scale of the house. It may be that a previous owner has raised the height in order to get rid of a downdraught and the stack looks unwieldy and out of proportion as a result. If you do not intend to use the fire you can restore the stack to its former height, but this will entail some research into regional forms if the restoration is to be true to the original.

It should be remembered that the use of modern heating appliances in an old chimney is apt to cause condensation as the products of combustion of certain fuels, mainly sulphuric acid, cause progressive deterioration of the brickwork and stain the outer walls. This can only be cured by completely relining the flue. In fact, chimneys built after 1965 were required by the new building regulations to be lined either with salt-glazed pipes or with some kind of precast liner. A

23 *A crumbling chimney stack which could be dangerous*

24 *Restoring Elizabethan chimneys to their original style, near Braintree, Essex. The chimneys are between 30 and 40 feet high. Flue liners are also being inserted*

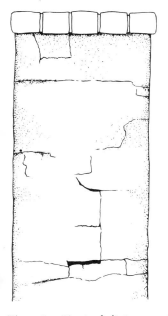

Fig. 18 *Typical disintegration of a chimney stack due to acid attack*

chimney built before that date can often be substantially improved by the use of a new lining system.

The development of the prefabricated chimney has brought great advances to flue efficiency and it has a life as long as the house itself. In addition to allowing the replacement of an existing chimney it means that an open fire can be introduced into a room where there is at present no chimney. This is particularly useful where an extension has been built on to an old cottage, as, for example, at Court Lees Cottage (Plate 4), where a new kitchen was added with a large wood-burning cooker installed in it. Without a prefabricated chimney it would have been difficult to use this type of heating and cooking stove without a further major building operation.

These chimneys are insulated with metal or ceramic liners to ensure even temperatures through the whole length of the flue, which means that the fires they serve will burn more brightly and there will be no chimney maintenance needed, apart from the occasional sweep.

The choice of heating appliance is important and there are many variations on old themes from which the restorer can choose to tie in with the particular period of the house he is restoring. These appliances are designed to burn either coal or smokeless fuel, but nowadays they usually carry some form of adjustment to regulate the air supply to the fire and so control the rate of burning.

The Solid Fuel Advisory Service gives free, unbiased information, advice and technical assistance to members of the public on how to heat the home efficiently. The National Fireplace Council has as its constituent members four major organizations, working together to form a fully comprehensive service. They have set up National Fireplace Centres in many cities and towns where the customer can be put in touch with specific manufacturers and where advice is freely given on all matters connected with fireplaces.

All in all, the restoration of an open fire in a period house has many advantages, not least the fact that a flue helps to ventilate a house and keep condensation to a minimum. This is a very important consideration in any old house. Most of all, an open fireplace makes us think again of 'log fires, lamplight and peace', which is no bad thing in this age of artificiality and high speed.

7
Windows and Joinery

One of the most interesting features about old houses is their variety of windows. Each period had its own type, true to character, fitting in with the general design of the building. For example, the Tudor period was characterized by the diamond-paned lattice on domestic buildings, a reminder of the early methods of filling in the 'wind hole' with a lattice of withies woven diagonally to allow the water to drain downwards. When glass became available in small flat pieces it was joined together by lead strips and the lights were separated by moulded mullions (upright posts). The use of glass was rare before the time of Henry VIII, except in a few great houses, wooden shutters being generally used to keep out the weather. It was not until the beginning of the Elizabethan period that windows were made to open and these were then in the shape of hand-wrought iron casements, made by the blacksmith and hung on hooks to the frame which was set in the timber framework of the house and fastened with ornamental fasteners.

The bay and oriel windows of the Perpendicular period developed into the large bays of Elizabethan and Jacobean houses, disappearing with the Restoration until their revival in Victorian days.

Sliding sash windows came into being towards the end of the seventeenth century and replaced the casement in all but the smallest houses, until the middle of the nineteenth century. At first they had thick glazing bars, with only the bottom half of the window capable of being opened. Later, the Georgian window became tall and dignified, with delicate wooden glazing bars in standard-sized panes of glass. It was one of the most aesthetically satisfying designs ever achieved, perfectly in scale with the architecture of the period. The design so caught on that many early sashes were replaced by the new type at different times, so one cannot date a house by means of its windows only.

During the Victorian period sash windows manipulated by pulleys and weights were in general use, some of those in larger houses carrying great sheets of heavy plate glass which nevertheless were so well balanced that they were easy to manoeuvre. Others were the twelve-pane double hung sash, with horns, which some people claim were most interesting. They had the effect of adding to the apparent size of the house, but a more practical reason for their preference was that if these smaller panes were broken they were easily and cheaply replaced.

The Edwardians in general preferred casements, particularly for country houses, hung to stone or solid wooden frames. On a long low building they gave a look of repose and harmony that reflected the pervading spirit of that more leisurely age.

All of these designs play a very important part in the architecture of their period and it is a great mistake to replace them with out-of-period substitutes. Even where old windows are failing in their prime function of letting in light and air whilst excluding rain and draughts, it is still possible to restore them without destroying the character of a house or spoiling the look of the exterior.

There is no need to sacrifice comfort to aestheticism either, for there are many specialist firms which are skilled in just such restoration work and will apply modern amenities like draught-proofing and double glazing to old windows and french doors with no difficulty. It is worth remembering that double glazing is recommended as a security measure these days.

Its price depends on window size, on whether you do it yourself or have it done professionally, and on whether you want 'second windows' fitted to existing ones, or entirely new ones.

Sash windows will take secondary glazing in the form of sheets of glass fixed inside by clips, easy to install. They provide useful noise insulation for a house on a busy road.

At first sight double glazing may seem to be expensive, but against that is a considerable saving on heat loss and, consequently, lower heating bills, as well as more comfort in the home.

There have been many advances of late in this field and it is worthwhile making full inquiries from the relevant trade association as to the credentials of firms who claim to be specialists, for there are many cut-price 'cowboys' around, eager to cash in on a rising market.

If it is necessary, for any reason, to have complete replacements of old windows, they can be made to the design of the original which should be faithfully copied. Old types of glazing bars can be replaced by the simple method of giving the joiner samples or templates of the original moulding.

Occasionally it is both necessary and desirable to add one or two windows to an old house, particularly if it is one that faces north with

25   *A Victorian sash window, with horns, set in a three-hundred-year-old Cotswold stone cottage*

Fig. 19   *Old leaded light patterns*

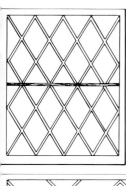

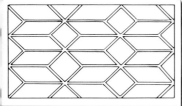

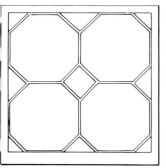

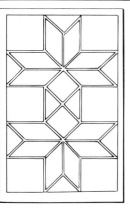

a comparatively windowless south wall. The reason for this may be that the early Elizabethans believed that the dreaded plague was borne on the south wind and they were afraid to let it into their houses. There may also be some bricked-in window spaces, the result of the window tax of 1695 which was not repealed until 1851. To avoid excessive payments many people filled in some of their windows, leaving behind a trail of blank spaces that can be seen to this day all over the country, more especially in Elizabethan farmhouses.

In these cases it is not a difficult matter to insert new windows and introduce more light from another aspect, but they should be in keeping with the design of the existing ones. A hotch-potch of designs will destroy any building's claim to authenticity.

The relationship of window space to wall surface can be varied to almost any extent provided the remaining features are in harmony, but windows robbed of their glazing bars (or, in earlier times, their lead lights) and glazed with one single sheet of glass destroy the whole balance and merely look like unfurnished gaps in the building.

As a rule there is no need for the approval of the local authority's planning department for replacement windows, provided that the window area is not being enlarged or that the new window does not substantially alter the appearance of the house. This would apply particularly if the house were of architectural interest, or a listed building, or in a conservation area. However, permission is required when opening up a new window or when putting in a bay window which would extend beyond the building line. If there is any doubt, the local planning departments are always pleased to advise.

It is worth remembering that tax relief is usually available on the interest paid on money borrowed for home improvements. If excessive noise is the reason for installing double glazed replacement windows, you might be eligible for a government grant towards the cost.

Leaded lights These are in a category of their own. Take them away, and the house or cottage would lose much of its charm and character. Their origin is way back in medieval times when the small diamond-paned lattice was generally used, but the Elizabethans and Jacobeans, with their exuberant taste in decoration, elaborated on the early designs and produced some more intricate patterns in lead glazing. Rather larger pieces of glass, often rectangular, were used for several later types of leaded lights up to the time of the Restoration, but then they disappeared until the time of the Victorian revival. They appeared again at the beginning of this century when the neo-Tudor style of house came into vogue.

Almost any period house, therefore, may have some leaded lights in it, very possibly including some historic or commemorative piece, probably coloured, which should be preserved.

The restorer may also come across some diamond-scratched message, or name, on an old pane, which may give an interesting insight into the history of the house. In Ardmaddy Castle, Argyllshire, there is a letter from a prisoner scratched on a window pane during the Jacobite rising of 1745. It is quite legible after almost two and a half centuries. I have come across many similar instances up and down the country.

Old or new techniques present no problems to the experienced craftsman. In the old days a craftsman used to buy old lead and melt it down, before putting it through a lead mill to produce the long strips necessary for glazing. Lead which has been milled in this way has milling teeth in the channel. Nowadays, it is extruded and bought in H-shaped sections, ready for use. For restoration work, the piece is taken apart and the glass thoroughly cleaned before remaking. Broken pieces are matched – although it is difficult to get a perfect match for the very early glass, there is still some very good 'antique' glass made. Many large windows had their small panes of glass supported by iron bars (saddle bars) fitted horizontally, about 12 to 18 inches apart and built into the window frame against the side of the window. The lead strips holding the glass (known as cambs, or cames) were secured to these bars to prevent bulging. Where the saddle bars are absent and the leads have become 'bowed' they can be repaired by inserting reinforcing steel bars through the cambs, but it is necessary to take the leads apart to do this.

It is possible to repair an odd small pane on site without removing a window, but more extensive damage is best tackled in the workshop where it can be flattened out on a bench to make sure that all joints are tight.

Any stained glass in an old house is apt to be valuable, if not a work of art. For example, in a small manor house in Kent there are four stained glass leaded lights in a window, of which three were the badges of Henry VIII and Catherine of Aragon. It transpired that the house was once the property of Henry VIII's standard-bearer and so has historic connections. This small window was one of the house's proudest possessions and very much cherished by the owners. The moral here seems to be that it is worthwhile establishing the value of any such glass before restoration, so that it can be treated with due care.

On the other hand, one can come across some very nondescript pieces which have been patched in as replacements at some time and may not warrant the expense of restoration. Anyone who is not sure should consult an expert before doing anything drastic.

In fact, restoring old stained glass is a job for the expert and no one else, for it is an ancient art. The use of coloured glass in windows can be traced back to the fifth century, and these early windows were all painted and formed by the mosaic method, using strikingly intense colours, ruby and blue predominating. Many specialized techniques were involved in their making and the subsequent complicated business of leading up, and the craftsman of today must be master of all these techniques and understand the traditional methods employed by his forebears in order to undertake restoration work successfully. It is wise to get in touch with a specialist firm for this delicate work – the ordinary glazier will not do. Where necessary, the Worshipful Company of Glaziers will supply the names of craftsmen.

True, it is more costly in the beginning to have leaded lights, plain or coloured; but set against that, the cost of repairing and replacing a pane is considerably less than the price of a picture window, for example, which would only be an anachronism in an old house.

Crown glass   All old glass is valuable and should be most carefully protected from damage while any building work is going on. Window glass was once commonly known as 'crown glass', that is, glass made in large circular discs by blowing and spinning round into a flat plate. The lump left in the plate where the glass had been attached to it was known as a 'bottle end' or a 'bull's eye'. Originally these were reckoned to be the most inferior part of the sheet and were used in cottages, for the most part, until they became fashionable in Regency days, when a good many were bought from old cottages for reuse in good houses.

In some towns many Georgian houses have retained the original crown glass in their sash windows, and no substitute, however good, could ever take their place.

There are some regional-style windows, which are peculiar to certain areas and vernacular buildings. One particularly attractive design is the graceful oriel window which, by no means restricted to any one area, still lends itself to a variety of decorative treatments in different areas.

During the nineteenth century curved bow windows came into fashion and some towns still have any number of local varieties, delightful to see. We should be infinitely poorer as a nation without the survival of such charming architectural features.

Window furniture This is a highly important detail which needs careful study if a true picture of a period is to be presented, for the type of latch or fastener used varies in different regions. Any original catches, latches or bars should be retained. Where they are missing a county museum will be able to supply specialized information concerning the types used. Such museums often display the items that were used in its area throughout all periods, so that they can be studied and reproduced during restoration.

Joinery The woodwork surrounding windows comes within the province of the joiner and not the glazier, and there are a number of interesting features to be considered in this respect.

Shutters are invariably worth retaining, for a number of reasons. They look attractive, they ensure privacy, they are an excellent insulation and they add to the security of a house. In some houses, particularly Regency and early nineteenth century ones, it may be found that internal shutters have been pinned back to deep window splays. In this case they should be freed, even if they are not wanted for everyday use, and any old panelling or mouldings, including splay or soffit panels (that is, the visible underside of a projecting surface), should be restored at the same time. Interior window sills should also be cleaned up and repaired where necessary, and anyone lucky enough to discover a window seat should keep it at all costs. There may be traces of some which have been concealed at some time in the history of the house. If so, they are worth reinstating, for these seats are both practical and pleasant.

Any old joinery is usually well worth saving and, as a rule, it is not difficult to repair. Basically, it is a matter of cutting out rotten sections of woodwork, piecing in new wood of the same kind and jointing it home securely.

There are several kinds of joints which may be used in woodwork generally and it is useful to have a working knowledge of them, both for structural work and repairs. Technical details are supplied in the captions to Figs. 20 and 21 and should cover all contingencies.

Timber floors Floors in old buildings were most likely of oak or elm, with wide boards. Because they are subject to constant wear and tear, they may have been renewed more than once. It is not unusual to find some damaged boarding which has at some time been cased with new deal, with the old rotted woodwork left as a source of hidden trouble. In some cases, two or three floors have been laid one upon another and these should now be opened up and repaired. In fact, an old house or

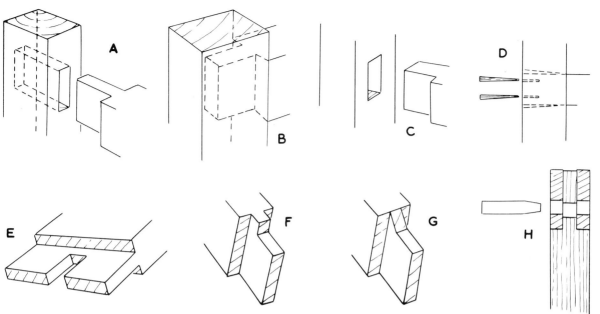

Fig. 20   *Mortise and tenon joints. It is usual for the tenon to be about one third of the thickness of the wood on which it is cut (A). If the appearance of a through tenon would be unacceptable on the surface, it may be cut short, and then becomes a 'stub' tenon in a 'blind' mortise (B). If the tenoned piece is narrower than the other, as in a rail crossing behind panelling in a door, it may be shouldered on one side only and is then a 'barefaced' tenon (C). In window frames and other assemblies, a tenon may be tightened with one or more wedges. It is stronger if the wedges go into cuts in the end of the tenon and expand it (D). If the tenoned piece is wide, weakening of the other part by cutting too long a mortise is avoided by having two or more tenons with a short haunch between (E). At a corner, an open mortise is avoided by cutting back the width of a tenon, but it is usual to provide a short haunch (F). A haunch can be cut at an angle so that it still provides some glue area but cannot be seen (G). In much traditional construction, mortise and tenon joints were strengthened with pegs driven across. They may still be used, but the strongest joint comes from drilling the tenon slightly closer to the shoulder than the hole through the mortised part. When a plug with a tapered end is driven in it draws the parts close together (H)*

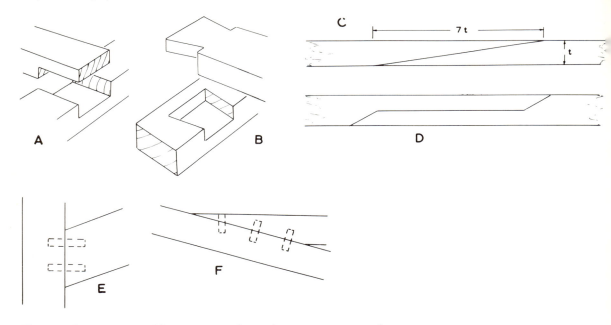

Fig. 21   *Repair joints. If two pieces of wood meet or cross at the
same level, half may be cut from each piece to make a half-lap
joint (A). A T-halving joint can be 'stopped' so that the end grain
does not show on the surface. If a resistance to pulling apart is
required, one or both sides of the joint can be cut at a dovetail
angle (B). It is possible to rely on plain glued joints, without shaped
parts. If two pieces are to be joined to make up length, as when a
broken part has to be cut away and a new piece joined on, the ends
may be spliced. No glue holds well on end grain, but if both parts
are cut to slopes of at least one in seven, the wood is sufficiently side-
grained to make a strong bond (C). There are several end-to-end
joints, but if the parts have to join without much endwise load, as
in extending a wall plate along brickwork for a roof extension,
they may notch over each other. It is better to avoid an abrupt
change of section by cutting ends at a slope instead of squarely
(D). In some modern work glued dowels are used where mortise
and tenon or other joints might have been employed. There
should be at least two in each joint and they should provide a
glue area comparable to the tenons that would otherwise have
been cut (E). An advantage of dowels is that they can have their
grain square to the meeting surfaces, where a tenon might be
almost cross-grained in an acutely angled meeting (F)*

cottage may be all the better for having its floors up, whatever the reason, for in so doing, the accumulated dust and rubbish of the years can be cleared away. Corners which are usually inaccessible can be ventilated and cleaned and any serious defects will come to light in this way.

A floor which has dropped, leaving a gap between the boarding and the skirtings, may indicate the presence of dry rot and this should be investigated without delay. To begin with, a small area of damaged flooring can be cut out by drilling holes about half an inch in diameter, an inch or so from where you judge the joist to be. Then, using a pad saw or hand-operated jig saw, cut down parallel to the joist and cut out as many sections of flooring as you need (Fig. 22). For example, an area of 16 × 16 inches – say, three boards between joists at 18-inch centres – is adequate for a small access trap door into the foundations. If you do not get close enough to the joist with the first cut you can measure accurately to make a second cut close to the joist. This is also a useful measure for inspecting plumbing, wiring, etc. Before the

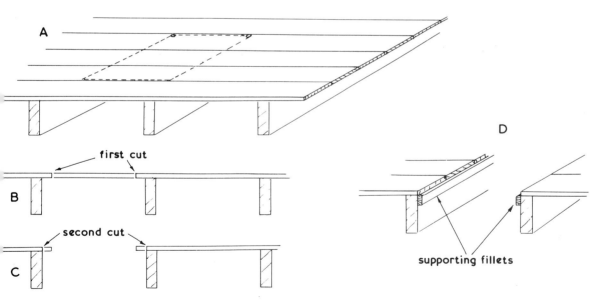

Fig. 22   *A. Preparing to cut out a small area of damaged flooring   B. First cut to find out position of joists   C. Second cut close to the joists   D. Supporting fillets fixed to the joists before boards are replaced*

boards are replaced they should be supported by fillets fixed on to the joists.

Where only part of the flooring needs to be replaced it may be necessary to use strips of $\frac{1}{8}$-inch hardboard to chock up modern $\frac{3}{4}$-inch flooring to the same height as the original 1-inch flooring (Fig. 23).

In repairing a timber floor it is important to treat each board individually, cutting away and piecing each one separately, taking care to preserve the continuous joint lines between the boards. Never patch across them: wood needs room to move and any movement and shrinkage must be restricted to the regular pattern of the original joint lines.

While boards are up take a good look at the joists below and the undersides of the boards to make sure that they are sound. If woodworm or rot is suspected, go over the timbers with a couple of coats of insecticide and rot fluid as a precautionary measure.

When boards have shrunk, leaving large gaps in between, it is best to have the floor taken up and relaid, with extra boards inserted where necessary, making sure they are butted together tightly. This is well worthwhile if the boards are in good condition.

Old skirting boards should be retained, repaired or replaced where necessary, with due regard to the original design, for they are needed to give a protective finish to the bottom of a wall where it meets the floor. Modern skirtings are dull and uninteresting, but in the past their design varied according to the period of a building and its quality. Some nineteenth-century houses had skirtings of considerable height, built up in sections, but the mouldings were fairly

Fig. 23　*Using strips of hardboard to chock up modern flooring to the same height as the original*

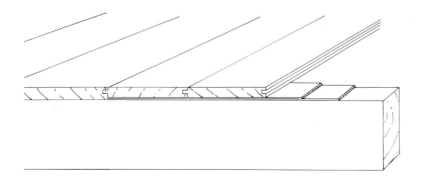

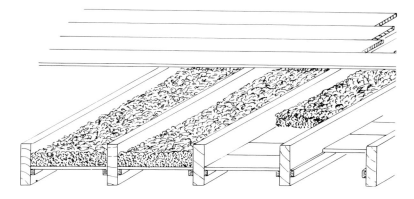

Fig. 24 *The Scottish method of 'deafening', or soundproofing, their Victorian houses consists of small rubble, ashes, etc., on boards half-way up between the joists. It is effective, but if damp penetrates it is difficult to dry out and therefore encourages dry rot*

simple and any joiner should be able to copy them for replacement purposes.

Old dados and chair rails are also interesting in a house of the appropriate period and should be retained where they are still good enough to warrant it.

In some very old houses there may still be a dado of original wainscot oak, which was one of the earliest forms of wall lining in the form of vertical oak boards, with edges overlapping or grooved into each other and fitted into horizontal beams top and bottom. It was used before true panelling was introduced. Sometimes a partition wall was built up in this way, using fine seasoned old oak. These linings are rare now, but not so rare are old matchboard partitions or dados which one sometimes comes across in nineteenth-century cottages. Matchboard simply means a board having a tongue along one edge and a corresponding groove on the other for fitting into similar boards. They were generally of softwood.

There is a similar kind of dado round the sitting room – once the schoolroom – of The Old School, Clanfield (Plate 14), and the owners have restored it to pristine condition. It is part of the atmosphere of the Victorian room and it is still useful to protect the walls where there are children around. Unless they are decayed beyond hope of saving, it

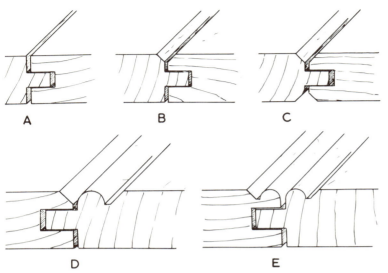

Fig. 25 *Matched boarding. If pieces of wood are to make up a broad panel, allowance has to be made for expansion and contraction in the widths of the boards and this may be done by using tongued and grooved matched boarding without glue in the joints. A plain joint (A) will show if shrinkage opens it, but that can be disguised by chamfering the meeting edges (B) including the second side if that will also be visible (C). If a bead is worked as well as the chamfer (D), any space left is even less obvious. A second bead may be used (E), but that may weaken the grooved edge*

is a pity to discard dados. In any case, they should be closely inspected, especially at the joints, and where any board needs replacing, take care to get the same kind of timber, well seasoned. An experienced joiner should be able to advise on these matters.

Other more decorative types of panelling come within the scope of the woodcarver and should probably be dealt with by him if they are at all valuable; but it is up to the householder to check the condition of any such timbers, making sure that they are free from any sign of rot or woodworm.

Careful inspection may also reveal something infinitely more interesting than woodworm. A panel that sounds hollow when tapped may turn out to be a concealed door, or jib door, set flush with the wall on both sides. Sometimes these doors were painted or papered over, to disguise them still more effectively. They should be set free so that their original purpose may be discovered. It is useless to speculate about them until they are opened up, but they may still serve a useful function today if the space behind is usable. Whatever they reveal, whether it be a secret cache or a hidden passage, their discovery will add one more facet to the history of the house.

Staircases   Stairs are an important architectural feature of any house and should be well protected while other work is going on. The treads of an old wooden staircase may show signs of wear and need to be strengthened from the underside, but if the framing itself is shaky the entire construction should be taken down and repaired. If repair is impossible, or impracticable, the original (if it is original) should be copied as nearly as possible, but make sure first that the staircase is not a later substitute, in which case you can feel free to have a new one designed, provided it is in keeping with the building. Also bear in mind that staircases had different plans in different periods.

A local joiner is usually capable of doing this work very competently, and in the case of a cottage staircase, for instance, it may be cheaper in the long run to have a new one made rather than have the old one repaired.

There are some architects who specialize in interior design and who will also design just the right staircase for a period house. It is surprising how this one feature, imaginatively used, can raise a house

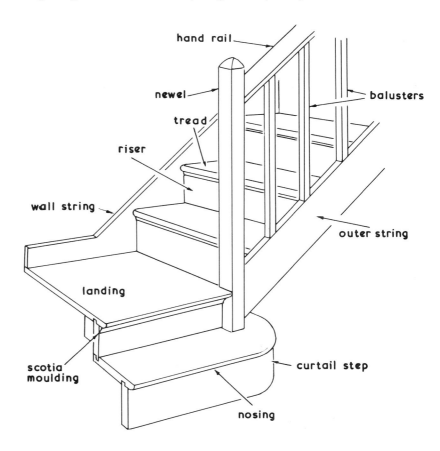

Fig. 26 *Parts of a staircase*

from the nondescript to the distinctive. It gives a hall a cheerful and inviting appearance to the visitor and leaves a parting guest full of pleasant recollections. A cantilevered geometric staircase with cast- or wrought-iron balusters, for example, looks dignified and graceful in the right setting – usually a nineteenth-century house of some size. This kind of staircase was quite prolific in Victorian days, especially in Scottish houses. The ironwork should be painted either black or white – never other colours – but it needs patience and a fine brush to paint the details of some of the beautiful designs in wrought iron that one sees around.

Balusters, newels, handrails, etc., should be kept to their original design and materials, whatever they may be. It is a mistake to apply paint to those parts of a staircase which look better in natural polished wood. What looks better than a gleaming polished mahogany handrail? If it has become splashed with paint and looks shabby it is worth taking trouble to clean it off and repolish it rather than paint over it.

If a new handrail, balusters or newel post are needed, a little research into the design and materials used in that period will pay dividends, for there may even be some local custom which the old-time builders followed, which is part of the vernacular architecture.

There may be cases where it is more convenient to resite the main staircase, without, of course, spoiling the plan of the building. Sometimes this can be an improvement, giving more light and space, but first, all the implications of such a move should be studied, with ample allowance made for turns and headroom.

A previous restorer may have panelled in a staircase in a mistaken attempt to modernize it or to save work. Usually this only succeeds in blocking out light to a lower hall and it looks out of tune in a period house. The panelling is generally of hardboard, which is simple to remove. The exposed balusters can then be stripped down to the original wood, which will most likely be pine. If this is so, they will look their best when sealed and polished. Where any balusters are badly damaged, they can be copied by a skilled wood turner, giving him an original to use as a pattern for replacements. The traditional type of cottage staircase with winder steps, however, should not be altered. This is usually completely enclosed with a boarded partition, with a handrail fixed to the wall. It is shut off at the bottom with a door. These staircases are best left alone, as part of the cottage design. Anything else would look out of place and contrived.

When designing a new staircase for an old house bear in mind that the requirements of the building regulations could well make certain kinds impossible. It is best to get acquainted with the regulations before embarking on any alterations.

Doors   Doors are obviously a very important part of a building and their design also reflects the period in which the house was built, unless – as may so often happen – someone has replaced original doors with others of unsuitable design. Nothing looks more out of place than a modern glass door in a Tudor cottage, for example, yet this is an anachronism perpetrated again and again, to the detriment of the old building.

Original doors should be retained and repaired wherever possible, and where there is any doubt about their design, take trouble to research in books, in museums of old buildings and other places, to ascertain exactly what type is suitable for your period house or cottage. You can also look for authentic examples in other houses, observing the doors, frames and architraves which are in keeping, and paying special attention to the mouldings and details of door cases.

As a rough guide, medieval outer doors were simply made of two layers of stout planks, vertical outside, horizontal inside, at first fastened together with wooden pegs, later with large hand-made iron nails with big stud heads in regular patterns, and straightened with

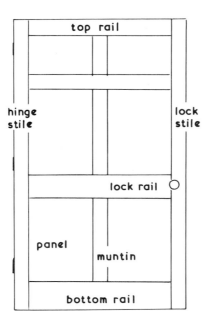
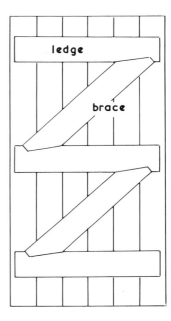

Fig. 27   *Parts of a door*

heavy iron hinges and straps. Many doors had vertical outer boards backed with only two or three horizontal boards ('battens' or 'ledges') spaced some distance apart. In the sixteenth century, a framed and panelled construction replaced the heavy boarding in more settled areas, its design following that of contemporary wall panelling up to the end of the eighteenth century. Also, there were pairs of narrow doors in one doorway in similar patterns (Plate 27). Door design followed the caprices of fashion and individual taste through the nineteenth century when four panels were often used and designs became increasingly elaborate for the main entrance door. However, the ledged types were still in use for smaller houses and cottages.

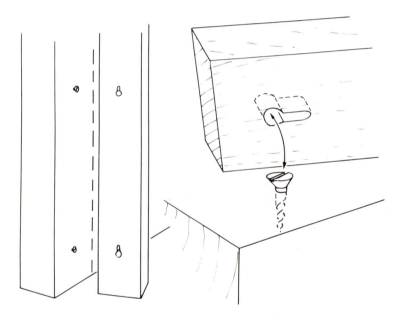

Fig. 28   *Secret slot screwing. This is used for attaching wood, such as a new architrave round a door, without screw heads showing on the surface. Screws are driven so that little more than their heads project. At each position in the other piece of wood there is a hole to clear the head and a slot to clear the neck of the screw, leading to the final position. The heads are inserted in the holes and the board driven along so that the screw heads cut along the bottom of the slots*

26 *A Tudor oak plank door, with concealed joins, in Town House, Great Bardfield*

27 *An eighteenth-century double door, with brass door furniture in keeping with the period*

Of course, there were exceptions in all periods, with more or fewer panels used according to whim, but so far as restoration is concerned the main aim should be, as always, to keep in period, remembering the type of building, whether it is a small cottage or grand house, for which you are planning.

When repairing an old ledged door, every effort should be made to obtain old mature hardwood boards that match the original. Traditionally, ledges were fixed to door planks with nails driven through the wood and clenched over, and this is the correct method to use. Some early doors may have the marks of the carpenter's adze on them, left as he faced up his timbers, following the fibre of the wood and making the finished effect as smooth as if a plane had been used, yet leaving a pleasantly undulating surface to the timber. This can rarely be imitated today, unless by an expert who really knows how to finish timber in this way, but bad fakes should be avoided at all costs.

If a restorer wants to replace an old door in its entirety he can either get one made up to the original pattern by a joiner, or he can search for the right replacement when old buildings of a similar period are being demolished. Demolition firms are usually very co-operative in this respect and many a prize has been won in this way.

When a complete new door is needed for a new opening, take care that it is the right size and in keeping with the scale and proportions of the room. Sizes were by no means standard in old houses.

Door furniture The methods of hanging old doors varied, with different types of hinge used in different periods. There were variations of the strap hinge up to the sixteenth century, followed by types of H and L hinge. Traditionally, these were nailed to the doors and frames, not screwed. The panelled doors of the eighteenth and nineteenth century used brass butt hinges, sometimes with a little decorative finish to the pins. All these original types should be preserved very carefully, together with old locks, keys and handles. Anything but a thumb latch on a ledged and braced cottage door would look wrong, or a drop ring handle on a sixteenth-century ledge door, or a Victorian Gothic door. Brass rim locks look right in more formal houses of the seventeenth and eighteenth centuries, and brass, china or wooden knobs suit the panelled doors of nineteenth-century houses.

Brass lever handles were used for eighteenth- and nineteenth-century panelled doors, especially where they were hung in pairs (Plate 27), and plain and stamped steel rim locks and latches with plain brass knobs were used for cottages.

There are, of course, variations on all these types, and there will undoubtedly be some styles peculiar to a locality or region, but a local blacksmith should know this, and be able to supply or restore any missing parts to the original design. It is worth having these items made up by a professional rather than spoiling the appearance of a door with a modern plastic handle or some such anachronism.

Woodcarving A full architectural joinery service should include the restoration of old woodcarvings as well as the more routine type of work.

Timber, being a natural material, is decorative enough in grain and texture, especially when hand-worked. There was some beautiful carving done in medieval days, particularly on timber-framed buildings, which gave even the smallest house a dignity and rare beauty of its own. Many regional characteristics were applied to decoration in timber but, generally speaking, the first decoration was the simple chamfer – the slanting face formed by cutting off an external angle – which was sometimes hollow or moulded. Corner posts and brackets were often singled out for more elaborate decoration, as were beams, doorways and porches. All sorts of designs were used, from flowers, foliage and the trailing vine to intricately carved figures, some displaying a symbolism which is incomprehensible to us now, although its very exuberance reveals the obvious joy the woodcarver had in his craft.

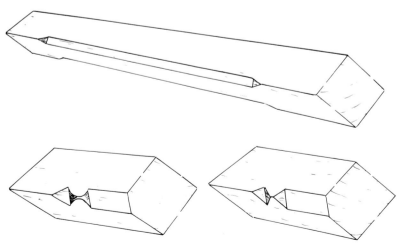

Fig. 29 *Chamfers. Where there is an angle between faces of a piece of wood exposed, the sharp edge, or 'arris', may be taken off by a bevel or chamfer, which can go the full length or, more often, be stopped with a simple sloping cut or a decorative pattern. On the underside of an old beam, which probably shows signs of being pitsawn, the chamfer should show the slight unevenness of being cut with an adze, and the end decoration of having been cut with a drawknife*

In Tudor buildings walls often had panelling carved in a vertical moulding known as linen-fold from its appearance. It was used on walls and doors alike. The Elizabethans used a simpler style of squared-up panels some 10 to 14 inches wide and 11 to 15 inches high. It was well proportioned, with the wood carefully chosen for its grain, a simple style that remained almost standard for about a century and is still repeated to this day.

Houses of the Georgian period have the kind of embellishment and decoration that the Adam brothers made famous over two hundred years ago. Theirs was the age of grace and delicacy, renowned for the work of the great master carver, Grinling Gibbon, who eventually left us a legacy of beautiful designs that have been the inspiration of woodcarvers ever since.

Today's craftsmen combine the traditions of the past with up-to-date scientific knowledge; they have to be even more versatile. They are just as likely to be called upon to restore medieval buildings abounding with old oak beams and posts enriched with symbolic figures as they are to carve foliage and festoon work after the manner of Gibbon – or, of course, to produce their own designs. As well as a knowledge of the old masters and their techniques they must have an exhaustive knowledge of timber in order to be able to match woods of the same age, grade, colour and texture of grain for restoration work. Their work often entails building up an entirely new part with nothing more than photographs or drawings to go on. For this the

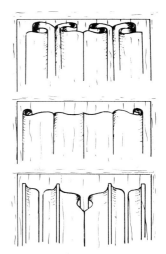

Fig. 30. *Types of linen-fold panelling*

craftsman must keep a supply of well-seasoned old oak, or any other wood that is required to match the original.

Sometimes the timbers of an old piece have to be cleaned thoroughly before the original can be appreciated. As well as corroding dirt, one or more coats of paint may be clogging the fine details of a period carving. Where the work has to be gilded, a special treatment is needed, with a final burnishing to restore the antique appearance. All these techniques are highly skilled and hardly come within the province of the unskilled amateur.

There are not many today who maintain the high traditions and craftsmanship of the old English woodcarvers, but where there is unique restoration work to be done, it is worthwhile seeking out the right man for the job.

8
Restoring Plasterwork

Plaster has been used, both externally and internally, for at least a thousand years. Although all kinds of plaster basically stem from limestone, there have been many developments over the years resulting in the use of many different kinds of plaster, any of which may be found in old houses.

Medieval walls were frequently intended to take either a thin coat of plaster or many thick coats of limewash and any renewal of the plasterwork should follow the pattern of the original, with no attempt made to correct the irregularity of the wall surface. Patching a defective area is never successful, since it will always show and is bound to weather differently. It is better to render a whole wall after a thorough clean down.

For old buildings, where there is unlikely to be a damp-proof course, limewash is still the best because it is porous and allows any dampness to dry out. Before renewing, the surface should first be dry-scraped to remove all loose and flaking limewash, then well scrubbed with a bristle brush. Where there has been any dampness or mould growth the walls should be washed down with a chemical solution containing a mould inhibitor, which should be allowed to dry on the surface before the new limewash is applied. Nowadays 'stone lime' can be bought easily.

Colour washes are prevalent in East Anglia and look very pleasant, but they should be in pale shades. Many of the modern colour washes are water-repellent, which gives additional protection to an outer wall, but where damp penetration is suspected a coat of anti-damp silicone applied to the walls before painting will often cure the trouble. Make sure that the wall has been thoroughly dried out first, or you will be sealing the moisture into it, with no escape route.

Stucco Stucco largely replaced the old lime and hair plaster towards the end of the eighteenth century, when the Regency builders were trying to find a rendering that was longer-lasting and more water-proof. They discovered 'cement plaster', or stucco, which is fine in texture, extremely hard and durable, and made to simulate stone. Thereafter, many buildings were faced with this material, often marked out in a masonry pattern with graphite. In fact, the London Building Act of 1774 advocated the use of stucco as a facing for buildings. It takes paint well, and with a smooth glossy finish in a neutral colour it looks very agreeable and is easy to maintain.

Interior plaster   Internal plastering that has lost its strength and has disintegrated needs to be stripped and entirely renewed. Lime should be used and not cement as the latter does not suit old walls and is apt to cause condensation. If the walls have been battened for lath and plaster construction the fault may lie in the failure of the battens, either through tannic acid attack on their fixing nails, or through rot and pests. In this case the battens should be renewed and, incidentally, there is nothing better than this to produce dry rooms, since the air space between the battens is an excellent insulation.

When the plaster is renewed, care should be taken to undercut any adjoining old work to dovetailed, clean edges, so that it is keyed in as much as possible.

Fig. 31   *A lath and plaster wall showing signs of disintegration*

Wall paintings Scraping down an old wall for renewal may reveal some far more welcome finds than rot, for the Tudors had a liking for painted murals. It is possible that the paintings were done by itinerant artists who left little or no evidence of their identity. Genuine examples are becoming rare, but restoration has uncovered some interesting ones. A favourite place for these paintings was above the fireplace, and two of this kind were discovered in a fifteenth-century timber-framed house in Teynham, Kent. One was an exceptionally fine painting of the royal coat of arms, supported by the English lion and the Welsh dragon of the Tudors, with a free-flowing design of fruit and birds in the background. It had been limewashed over with the date 1688 scratched on it, and although it took a winter's painstaking work to restore it to its Elizabethan splendour, the owners were highly delighted with the result.

The exposing and repair of wall paintings is a specialized job which many people may not feel able to undertake, but the names of recommended experts in this field are obtainable from such bodies as the Society for the Protection of Ancient Buildings. It is always worth contacting them in these cases, where something historic may be at stake.

Decorative plasterwork There is, as a rule, some very interesting decorative plasterwork in the interior of period houses. Some beautifully moulded ceilings and cornices were installed in all types of houses – small and large – up to and including the Victorian period. Where they have been taken away, the house looks bare and 'undressed' and, inevitably, has lost some of its character.

In all periods the plaster ornamentation complemented the style of architecture and bore a close relationship to the work of woodcarvers, stonemasons and sculptors. All were expressing the spirit of the age in their own medium. Restoration, in this sense, is re-creating history and the restorer must have a knowledge of the techniques that were involved and the materials that were used.

The craftsman in this field works in 'fibrous plaster', more commonly known as plaster of Paris, after the place of its origin. It is usually reinforced with jute rag and has enormous strength once it is set. At the same time, it is adaptable, ideal for restoration work.

Old houses are likely to contain plasterwork of all kinds, from the characteristic bosses and emblems of the Tudor period, the heavy plaster pendants and elaborate friezes of the Jacobeans, the enriched mouldings of the Renaissance, the rococo type of decoration of the mid eighteenth century, the delicate geometric designs of Adam, to

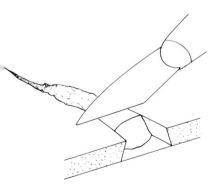

Fig. 32 *Patching plaster. If a crack or other flaw in plasterwork has to be filled, scrape it out so that it is undercut, with a greater width at the bottom*

the more complicated style of the Victorians. It is important, therefore, to appreciate the period of a building and the kind of workmanship that was put into it.

For example, the elaborately ribbed and moulded plaster ceilings of the sixteenth and seventeenth centuries were built up from members cast in moulds and put together on site, the heavy pendants generally being supported on lead strips. (Bits of wire and metal prongs can often be seen protruding from broken pieces of plaster.) Some of the most expensive work, particularly that of the eighteenth century, also involved deep undercutting, and on close inspection some of these early ornamentations modelled *in situ* look quite rough. The modern method of precasting and putting up in a unit actually makes for sharper detail and is therefore an improvement.

For restoration purposes anything that is already there can be imitated by taking moulds from the original. This is done by taking a clay 'squeeze', first covering the surface of the plaster with french

28   An early eighteenth-century moulded plaster ceiling in geometric design. The centre is typical of the period with a motif of curled-over acanthus leaves

chalk or grease before applying the clay. When the clay is pulled away there should be a full impression from which a mould can be made. This is the usual procedure where a small area is to be restored, but a large area might be removed and taken to the workshop to be moulded, with replacement sections cast there.

All loose material is stripped off the old plaster, which is given a coat of sealer before the new plaster is bedded on and stuck to the old. If a squeeze does not give the desired result the designer has to make dimension drawings from which he creates his own model. This depends, of course, on the expert's assessment, but a good deal is done by measuring and investigating beforehand.

The conscientious restorer should make sure that original plaster ceiling mouldings, cornices, etc., are carefully preserved, no matter what part of the house they may happen to be in. When dividing rooms in old houses he should avoid cutting across plasterwork decoration wherever possible. If this cannot be done with any degree of success, then any timber or plaster cornices should be continued along the new partition walls. This may be expensive but it is necessary, particularly where valuable old plasterwork is concerned. Besides, a room would look very odd and unfinished without this continuity.

On the whole, restoration in this area is not a job for the do-it-yourself enthusiast, and the ordinary householder is not recommended to do any more than clean up or repaint his plasterwork. It should simply be washed thoroughly with a fairly strong detergent to make sure that all dirt and grease are removed before fresh paint is applied, but the painter needs a very delicate touch if the ornamentation is to be kept crisp and clearly defined. A white emulsion paint is generally used, though this would not have been used, say, in the eighteenth century, so if the work is very important it is worth researching the type of paint which might originally have been used.

The amateur is strongly advised not to attempt anything more ambitious than this cleaning and painting. Where anything of historic or intrinsic value is concerned, it pays to consult the expert every time.

Some of the ornamental plasterwork ceilings to be seen in stately homes are beautiful works of art, and to quote Horace Walpole at the opening of Norfolk House in 1756, 'One can spend much time gazing in the air at the delightful ceilings.'

While we can enjoy looking at them, few of us these days can afford to restore or reinstate them in their original elaborate form, and in this context we owe much to those commercial organizations that are taking over old buildings and restoring them to the original. They are doing a national service, and keeping old crafts alive.

Nevertheless, there are some old houses which, having been denuded of their plaster decorations for some reason, still cry out for this form of relief ornamentation to set the tone of a room. Happily, for many, there is now an alternative to fibrous plaster in the form of rigid polyurethane, which is a hard, virtually unbreakable material. Ceiling roses, cornices and other mouldings can be reproduced in traditional designs which are indistinguishable from the plaster originals when fitted. However, care should be taken that they are the right pattern for the house and a little preliminary research in this field may be necessary before making a choice. These ornamentations are a reasonable price, easily fixed, and the white finish in which they are supplied is an ideal undercoat for any subsequent decoration.

The purists may quibble, but the ultimate answer lies in the quality and beauty of the mouldings themselves, and how well they meet the need of the average householder.

Pargeting   External plasterwork was not always left plain and featureless and in some cases vied with the interior work for sheer beauty and luxuriance of design.

There was some interesting work done in varying forms, the most distinctive of which is known as pargeting. It is seldom seen outside a certain limited area in the eastern counties, and some say this is because it originated from Low Countries craftsmen who settled in these parts and brought their skills with them.

There are two types of this decoration, one incised and one in relief. In the early days the patterns were in the form of signs or symbols, a sop to superstition. They were carved with a pointed stick while the plaster was still wet, giving little more than an added texture to the surface. Then came the traditional pricked or combed patterns seen on cottages today, in the form of semi-circles, scallops or oyster shells, crows' feet, cables, herringbone and the chevron. From this simple incised pargeting developed the ornamentation in relief that seems to bear some relationship to sculpture and woodcarving.

Much of the finest work in this idiom stems from the seventeenth century when the craft was at its peak, and the results of the unrestrained exuberance of the old-time craftsmen can be seen on many East Anglian buildings today – beautiful designs in high relief, amazingly detailed and lifelike in effect, but needing care to maintain them in good condition.

In common with other plasterwork pargeting gets dirty, especially in the present-day polluted atmosphere. Repainting, or applying another coat of limewash or colourwash, is apt to blur the outlines

29 *Pargeting on the old Clergy House, Clare, Suffolk. It is up to 4 inches proud of the wall, and was restored by a local craftsman*

and some of the original crispness is lost. When this treatment is repeated a few times the plaster becomes heavy, with the result that the wall is no longer able to carry it and pieces fall away. This is one of the main causes of its destruction; the other is sheer neglect. But it need not be lost for ever, because there are rural craftsmen available who are supremely capable of restoring this beautiful sculptured plasterwork.

I came across one of these fine old craftsmen in Clare, Suffolk, and such was his reputation that he had been entrusted with the restoration of the exterior of a house for the Ministry of Works – exacting, intricate work, for much of which he had to rely on photographs to show the original relief design.

The work is carried out with simple home-made tools which the craftsmen very often make in their own workshops, and their raw material is the plaster which has to be mixed with a thoroughness that leaves no room for error. This plaster used to be made of slaked lime, sand and finely teased horse or cow hair, cleaned of all dirt. The memory of this hard and tedious work is invariably the old-timers' earliest boyhood recollection, when they worked long hours for a pittance. It is difficult to get animal hair now so they use chaff as a binding agent.

The pargeting is done by floating a thick coat of plaster on to a 'keyed' base, using a wooden mould to mark out the panels. The work has to be done very quickly, while the plaster is wet, to avoid any cracking. If that happens, the whole surface has to be done again. For patterns like the oyster shell or scallop, a short pronged comb is used, but more intricate designs are outlined first in freehand, then 'backed up' with a pointed trowel to project them in relief. Centres of flower petals and similar designs are hollowed out with the back of a spoon of appropriate size, and a table fork comes in handy to rough up any contrasting parts. The finishing is done with a piece of wet rag or a small paintbrush dipped in water to smooth up the surface.

To a large extent, the pargeters of today are obliged to adopt new methods, such as the use of expanded metal instead of riven laths on which to float the plaster sheath, for the old ways involve too much time and labour, inevitably making them too costly.

Nevertheless, in spite of the problems of economics the craft remains virtually unchanged, for nothing can take the place of the skilled and sensitive hands of the artist-craftsman. It is right that we should cherish and renew the examples of ornamental pargeting that we have left to us and reproduce what has already been destroyed wherever possible.

9
Metalwork

Nearly all period houses possess some kind of metalwork which justifies restoration. Such things as ornamental leadwork, medieval hinge and key plates, latches, window fasteners, stud heads and other items which may vary with different regions, all have their part to play in giving a house its own distinctive flavour. It can be immensely interesting and rewarding to search out these small items where they are missing, finding out the local styles and bringing them back into use once more.

Lead Original lead is, of course, very valuable. It used to be used on roofs because it is such an excellent material for repelling water and it is inflammable. For a long time it was the only material that could be used externally on flat, or nearly flat roofs, but it has long been superseded by less expensive materials. However, if an old house has a small expanse of lead roofing that is wearing thin due to oxidation, it can either be patched or the old lead can be recast, using a certain amount of new lead with it, without creating undue problems.

What is far more likely nowadays is that the average householder may find himself the fortunate possessor of some original rainwater furniture, for lead was used for pipes, gutters and rainwater heads from about the middle of the Tudor period. It was often very decorative; even the ears holding the pipes in position against the wall were decorated, often with the heraldic motifs which the Tudors and the Elizabethans loved to use so freely. By the beginning of the eighteenth century some very ornate rainwater heads were cast in several pieces which had to be moulded together for fixing. Some of them had very attractive designs on them which gave a touch of pure artistry to that mundane, but necessary household feature, the drainpipe.

Sadly, the art of ornamental leadwork declined with the Palladians and after that period it remained to be seen only in garden statuary.

However, where such fine ornamental work still exists it can be preserved to a certain extent. Some of the larger mouldings which were used in rainwater heads tend to be heavy and their fixings need frequent checking to make sure they are fast and tight; if the metal is damaged it can be recast and made to look as good as the original. Damaged and dented pipes can be removed from their fixings and redressed, but other slighter damage may be repaired by lead burning. It is for the expert to advise.

Many householders like to paint their pipes, but it is as well to remember that paint will not adhere well to lead, and it is best left unpainted.

Wrought ironwork   Before the eighteenth century iron was all hand-wrought and most of the domestic work was given decorative forms. Between about 1700 and 1750 it was the fashion to have a wrought-iron staircase and balcony balustrading, gates and railings in various beautiful designs. A great many houses of this period possess some of these delightful features, which may well be the work of one of the seventeenth- or eighteenth-century masters of the craft, such as Jean Tijou, Robert Bakewell, Thomas Robinson and others, and should be properly restored at all costs.

30   *An old lead rainwater collecting box awaiting repair*

There is also plenty of inferior machine-made ironwork, probably replacing hand-made work, but this is not worth renovating. It is helpful, therefore, to be able to distinguish between them.

There are in fact certain glaring differences which even the uninitiated should be able to recognize; basically, they are to be seen in the scroll work, which forms the basis of practically all designs, adding strength as well as decoration to a structure.

Scrolls may be a 'C' or 'S' shape, simple or elaborate in their flowing curves. They give a quality of 'aliveness' and movement to the rigid verticals or horizontals into which they are fitted.

In hand-forged work the ends of scrolls are individually treated, either by tapering the metal down to the tip or by fashioning it into a leaf or other decorative forms known as snubs. The snub end is again treated in many different ways, a common characteristic being ends that are thickened into a solid knob instead of being drawn out.

The ends of these terminals have delightfully descriptive names, like ribbon-end, leaf-end, fish-tail, snub-end, halfpenny, and so on.

Another traditional type of decoration where handwork is evident is that of stylized leaves in the shape of water-lily leaves or harts' tongue ferns, requiring much skill to weld thin material to thick; but the most delicate and specialized work of all is repoussé. In this the embossed leaves are ribbed, veined and raised by hand forging with a host of small rodded hand tools, which are used in conjunction with suitably shaped stakes to support the work while the detailed impression is made from the top. It is a method that dates back to the twelfth century, and when it is skilfully carried out the result is uncannily lifelike.

The component parts of a piece are forged and fastened together with the use of rivets and collars, or by pinning, screwing and bolting, but where two or more pieces branch from each other a gracefully blending 'flow in' is produced by hammering the metal together while it is hot enough to be malleable.

In cheaper mass-produced work all these signs of craftsmanship are missing. Leaves are stamped out by machine, scrolls are made to terminate abruptly with a chopped-off appearance, collars are left off and the work is electrically arc-welded together. If it is not thoroughly cleaned off by grinding there will be blemishes left on it – a smith would call it 'polluted'.

Sometimes there is an obvious attempt to disguise an inferior piece of work by making hammer bruises to produce the effect of hand forging, but this is quite wrong, for the best wrought ironwork is free from disfigurement of any kind.

Time and neglect take their toll of ironwork such as this. If left without any kind of maintenance it becomes scaled and rusted, or it may be thickly encrusted with many layers of paint with which someone has sought to conceal the damage. In fact, it does nothing but conceal the fine workmanship.

To restore it, the first thing to be done is to clean up the piece and assess the damage. A suitable stripping agent may safely be used to remove flaking paint, but the iron is normally cleansed of scale and rust by chipping, scraping and hard wire brushing. If it is extensively corroded it may need to be burnt off in order to get down to the clean metal, and then it should be given a good-quality oxide primer immediately. This should be followed by two undercoats of a good-quality paint and two top coats. This is the ideal, as recommended by an experienced smith.

Traditionally, top coats should be flat black (Berlin black) but this does not have very good weathering qualities for external work. Eggshell or glossy paint is much better for shedding water.

In general, artificial colouring spoils the natural look of iron and should be avoided. Great care should be taken with the painting at all stages, or the fine detail of the work will be lost. To quote an old smith: 'It shouldn't be slopped on anyhow.' Ideally, painting should be done every five years to prevent corrosion. If this is done regularly, ironwork will remain sound for centuries.

There is a good opportunity to paint all wrought ironwork when it is dismantled for restoration. Iron casements, for example, should be well painted before fixing so that no part of the metal comes into contact with the corrosive influence of the tannic acid in the oak frames. It is an advantage to put a layer of some substantial anti-corrosive material between the casement and the frame. This will form an adequate barrier between the two and give additional protection. Where there is a large gap between the frame and the casement a twist of the same material can be inserted. This will also help to exclude draughts.

Painting is well within the scope of the amateur but repairs or restoration should be done by a blacksmith, one who is skilled in decorative wrought ironwork. Medieval work, such as hinges and key plates, are of great historic value and justify careful repair. Gates should be made to hang with free movement, and the hinge pins, fixings and furnishings made good.

The main objective of all restoration work is to keep as much of the original as possible. This, of course, depends upon how perfect the existing pieces are, but where the damage is beyond repair the pieces can be remade according to the original design, then welded on to the main part.

In some cases, a broken scroll can be repaired by making up the missing part and welding it on to the original, but often the entire scroll has to be remade. The blacksmith shapes his scrolls by eye alone, fashioning them on the beak and face of the anvil by hammer blows and nothing else. He heats the length of iron a little at a time, brushing off the dirt that comes out of the fire with a wire brush, or scratch brush, between each heating. This is the routine procedure to prevent dirt forming on the iron. He taps the red-hot bar lightly downwards with his hammer, then turns it over with the angled tip pointing upwards and taps it from the far side so that the tip folds over on itself to form the terminal, of whatever shape it may be. Again and again he reheats the iron until he has moulded it into the pattern he desires, using skill and judgement with regard to the proportions and curves. It looks easy to the untutored eye as one watches the smith working with quick, sure movements between anvil and the roaring fire. He knows to within a fraction of an inch just the right spot in the heat of the fire pit in which to hold and manipulate the piece of iron he is forging, and he knows exactly what he is going to do in the limited time he has to 'catch' the heat of the metal and strike it at the critical angle, all the time shaping it to measurements carried in his eye. Like all born craftsmen, he works by instinct, not scientific instruments.

31 *A wrought-iron gate at Preston-on-Stour, Warwickshire, restored by a local blacksmith. Many of the fine details were rusted and broken and had to be remade by hand forging*

On external work, it is usually the light, thin leaves that need attention first. They catch the water which encourages rust, and where this happens there is no alternative but to replace them. The smith does this by flattening out an old leaf to get the basic shape, then he cuts it out in a suitable thickness of material, shaping, moulding and forging until he has an exact replica of the original – 'So that it looks as if the wind has blown it!' a Warwickshire smith said.

A fine example of this smith's work is to be seen at Preston-on-Stour church, Warwickshire, where he restored gates made in about 1670 by Nicholas Paris of Warwick (Plate 31). The gates were in very poor condition with much of the ornamentation broken or rotted away. A good proportion of the overthrow and some of the scroll work were missing; some of the main bars and the dog bars at the bottom were broken; the hinge pins were worn and needed building up; many clips were broken and the locks had to be replaced. In addition, every leaf had to be remade to an exact copy of the original. It was a superb exercise in craftsmanship, and a permanent tribute to the smith who did it. For work like this on a grand scale the gates have to be taken down and put on a table in the smithy or on the floor.

Apart from the more costly items like gates, screens or balustrading, there are many smaller pieces made in wrought iron, such as knockers, bell pulls, wall brackets, porch lanterns, and so on, that are of exquisite design and well worth restoring or at least replacing.

32   *Detail of restored wrought-iron balustrading, a perfect replica of the original*

The country smith is always pleased to co-operate with the householder, or the architect, to produce, for example, the exact kind of key escutcheons, handles, handle plates, lock plates, hinges or similar fittings that are wanted to put the finishing touches to the restoration of an old house. Sometimes he makes a drawing of the original item first, but that depends upon the nature of the work. One may be certain that what he cannot restore he can reproduce.

Cast iron   Ironfounding is one of the ancient trades that tends to be regarded as industrial rather than decorative, but in fact the adaptability and versatility of iron make it a wonderful material to work for a number of purposes.

Long before the invention of the blast furnace small foundries were turning out some remarkably good decorative domestic ironwork, some of which survives to this day. (For those who are interested there is a collection of this early work shown at Anne of Cleves House, near Lewes, East Sussex.)

Towards the middle of the eighteenth century cast iron began to be used by architects for decorative as well as structural purposes and from that time onwards it achieved a new status and came to be regarded as an art medium alongside its sister craft of wrought ironwork. The Georgians produced some very beautiful castings for panels, balconies, balustrades, gates and so on, which are seen on many eighteenth-century houses as part of the whole dignified and elegant composition.

The Victorians also used cast iron freely on the domestic scene,

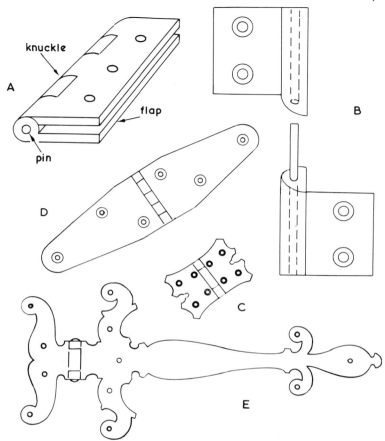

Fig. 33   *Types of hinges. The butt hinge is normally let into the wood between a door edge and its frame. The pin may finish level, as shown (A), or be continued into decorative knobs. A rising butt hinge is made to separate into two parts so that a door may be lifted off. The two sloping surfaces around the pin slide on each other so that the door lifts as it is opened, providing clearance for floor coverings (B). Another hinge serves the same purpose as a butt hinge, but is mounted on the surface and given a decorative outline (in this case Jacobean). There may be extra holes to give a wide spread of screws and a stronger joint (C). If the load is greater or the screws are to be spread into more boards, the choice is a strap hinge (D). If there is insufficient room for a strap both ways, as at a door frame, a T-hinge is used, like this Jacobean one (E)*

33   *An L-type iron hinge, often used in the seventeenth and eighteenth centuries. This one is fixed straight into the brick wall*

even having decorated foot scrapers, manhole lids, coalhole covers and other similar items that are now much sought after by collectors of Victoriana, as well as those restorers who seek to replace them.

For these articles we need to go to the small craftsman who is prepared to meet individual requirements. He is not an easy person to find in these days of mass production but he is worth seeking out.

It was in one of these small foundries that I was initiated into the mysteries of casting. Basically, the craftsmen were using the same methods as those used by the sixteenth-century ironfounders – that is, sand moulding and hand sculpting – the only concession to modernity being that a pattern is now used to save time with hand sculpting. A mould must conform exactly to the shape of the pattern and it must be absolutely uniform in structure, otherwise the enormous heat and pressure of the molten metal being poured into it would at once detect any flaws or hidden internal pockets, and the resulting casting would be useless.

The fascinating feature of this foundry was that it was using old iron, recycling it and converting it into molten metal to live again in the form of firebacks, fire irons and a host of other household items, both useful and decorative. The technical details of the transformation are interesting but have no particular relevance here. More important to the householder who is seeking to replace a lost or broken item is that with the traditional method of sand moulding there is no problem about producing the one-off article, whereas a great industrial foundry would need to produce several thousands of the same thing to make it pay. Small aluminium castings are made in the same way.

Original items are used for patterns where possible, but even a photograph will do. Clients sometimes take their own patterns to this foundry, particularly when they want a casting for some special purpose. Many strange objects have been made in this way. Where it is a case of restoring broken ironwork the best course is to have the broken pieces welded together to make a pattern, then recast. If it is just rusted and dirty, it can be restored by cleaning off all surface dirt and grease, brushing off any traces of rust with a wire brush until the bare clean metal is reached, and then a rust-inhibiting undercoat should be applied, followed by a metallic preservative paint, in much the same way as the procedure for wrought ironwork.

The work that is turned out by a small country foundry is usually highly individual. In comparison with mass-produced goods it is not expensive and in return one has an article of one's own choice rather than a dull and lifeless one of the type that is seen by the thousand in supermarkets.

There were other, less decorative articles, such as gutters and rainwater pipes, that were made in cast iron during the nineteenth century, and where these are still in evidence they need to be painted regularly. A black bituminous paint is the best for this job as it does not absorb water and is less permeable to water vapour. It should be applied on surfaces that are completely clean and dry, with all the rust and scale removed, and then it will adhere strongly, forming a tough coating resistant to corrosion even in extremely exposed conditions.

Cast-iron pipes and gutters which have been allowed to rust to the point where nothing can be done to restore them will have to be replaced. The question arises, with what? Nowadays, plastic gutterings and rainpipes are a good substitute and if properly fitted they merge in with any period of architecture quite well. They may be painted, if you wish, but they need not be, so the question of maintenance does not arise. A further point in their favour is that they are cheaper than any other form of rainwater furniture.

Brass Finally, on the subject of metalwork, you may come across some very fine brass door furniture in a Georgian house. Locks, handles and hinges were all, as a rule, beautifully made, with the same touch of elegance that is apparent in other fitments of that era. On the other hand, there are few fields in which so many crude, out-of-place 'reproductions' have been made, and the restorer should beware of being misled by slick sales talk. Suitable replacements which are authentic reproductions may be obtained from reputable architectural ironmongers.

34 *A Victorian wood-cased brass-bound lock that has been painted over. It could be made more attractive by stripping, cleaning and polishing*

IO
Preservation and General Care of the House

It is a waste of time and money to restore an old house in order to make it comfortable and habitable and then neglect to preserve it.

The subject of preservation covers a very wide field, but the main concern of the householder should be to protect his property from damp, timber pests, and wet and dry rot. These are the most worrying problems, but thanks to modern technology, they can be overcome in all cases once the warning signs are recognized.

Damp   As already emphasized, this is without doubt the arch-enemy of an old building. Its signs and symptoms are unmistakable and should have been noted at the preliminary inspection stage; the classic signs of damp and rising damp are set out in Chapter 1. The only way to preserve a house from its ravages is to install an efficient damp-proof course without delay. Few old houses were built with one yet they seem to have survived for hundreds of years unprotected in this way; but the developments that are always going on around us these days upset the natural drainage of the land over a wide area and may

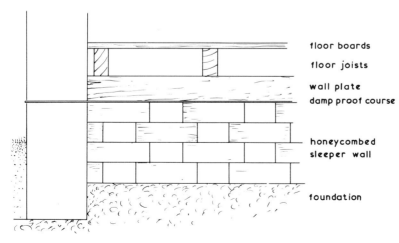

floor boards
floor joists
wall plate
damp proof course

honeycombed sleeper wall

foundation

Fig. 34 *Sleeper walls. If flooring is to be supported by brickwork inside a building, such sleeper walls should be honeycombed to allow a good circulation of air, and there should be air bricks in external walls*

result in rising damp in a house that has been relatively free up till now. Though modern building regulations insist upon a damp-proof course in new buildings, no such insistence exists with regard to old buildings, and it is up to the householder to be aware of this risk.

The conventional type of damp-proof course consists of horizontal membranes of some non-absorbent material fixed well above the surface of the ground to prevent moisture being drawn up into the walls by capillary attraction. Air bricks may also be inserted at intervals to ventilate the space beneath the floor.

There are many more modern methods of damp-proofing available today; for example, the silicone injection method into the walls, to create a course saturated with water-repellent resins. It is quick, clean and effective, but it may not be suitable for all types of houses, particularly timber-framed ones. The householder is advised to study all methods carefully and to consult a reputable specialist firm about this kind of problem. They have their expert technologists who will, if required, survey the property and give free advice.

Other first-aid methods used by householders to combat damp, such as digging a trench around the house or inserting a concrete raft, have already been mentioned (see Chapter 2), and the conclusion is that each case must be assessed individually. One cannot be too dogmatic about old houses. The main thing is to recognize the trouble. Damp won't just go away unless it is cured at source and it will cause unending problems while it exists.

Condensation, rather than damp, often causes a black mould to appear on a wall – a disfiguring blot which refuses to go even after the trouble is cured. In this case the paintwork should be scrubbed down and the affected wall coverings stripped off before treating the area with a proprietary fungicide.

Likewise, green mould on outside walls may not necessarily be a sign of damp. It could be an algae which grows in shade. Possibly an overgrown tree or a shrub is blocking the light from the wall and the algae will disappear if the offending growth is cut back. If this cannot be done the wall can be treated with a fungicide, and this will need to be repeated every few years.

Generally speaking, the standard cures for dampness and condensation are better heating and better ventilation. There must be a supply of fresh air into a room, if not through an open window then through an air brick. Condensation on glazing can sometimes be an intractable problem and there seems to be little that can be done to prevent it, but it should be ensured that the running moisture is diverted before it can cause any damage.

An old house will often contain cupboards without any kind of ventilation and these encourage damp and the formulation of mould. The answer is to fit a grille or to drill some air holes, top and bottom, at the sides.

Draughts are uncomfortable, but at the same time they provide ventilation of a kind. Where they are excessive, self-adhesive or metal strips round doors and window frames will help to keep them out. Double glazing is a certain cure. At the same time, one should avoid sealing a room so completely that the air becomes stagnant.

A successful cure for front-door draughts is the fitting of a porch. This was done very successfully at Cuilfail (Plate 35). The porch here was made of glass-reinforced plaster and was supplied in a kit. It was very easy to erect and has proved to be highly efficient. It adds to the classical appearance of the house and is a practical solution to

35 Cuilfail, Helensburgh, Dunbartonshire, showing the damp-proofing at ground level. The built-on porch is of glass-reinforced plaster. The wing at the west end is an addition after the house was built, and a false wall at the east side disguises a conservatory built on to the house

unwelcome draughts in an exposed and windy situation. In this sense, it is preserving the life of the house by giving added protection.

Insulation It is a mistake to be sparing with the heating in an old house, especially where it has a tendency to dampness, but at the same time the cost of energy is formidable. To cut down heating bills to reasonable levels it is wise to insulate wherever possible, and this applies particularly to the roof where hot air rises and escapes at the rate of 25 per cent.

There is a variety of insulating material from which to choose – glass fibre, mineral wool, expanded polystyrene or cork. All are equally efficient. They come in either rolls or sheets which can be laid down between the joists, or loose-fill granules which are poured between the joists to the requisite depth. These materials virtually act as a tea cosy, keeping the heat in. Always choose a reputable brand of material and follow the manufacturers' instructions carefully. Wear gloves and a face mask when handling them, as the fibres tend to irritate the skin.

The cold-water pipes and tank also need lagging as a protection against frost, and for this moulded plastic foam sleeving can be used for the pipes and cut sheets of insulation material or a jacket of glass-fibre matting for the tank. There is no need to insulate under the tank, as there will be some warmth rising through the floor to prevent the water getting too cold. The hot-water tank should be fitted with insulation too; a well-fitting thick jacket can be bought at a very reasonable price and takes less than twenty minutes to fit.

Generally speaking, the insulation of walls, whether they are of cavity or solid construction, is a job for the specialist, who will guarantee good results. If the walls need resurfacing externally or replastering internally the extra work and cost of insulation at the same time is worthwhile. It helps to reduce condensation and noise levels, as well as improving the warmth of the house.

Old houses often need a new ground floor and this is a good opportunity to insulate it by making a solid floor insulated with a chipboard and extruded polystyrene 'sandwich'. Upstairs floors need not be insulated as they benefit from rising heat.

All this, of course, depends upon the period of the house and the kind of insulation suited to it. On the whole, however, it makes good economic sense and will increase the value of any house while helping to preserve it.

Free advice and help on insulating a house of any kind can be obtained from any of the larger gas or electricity showrooms.

Rot – wet and dry Both these menaces are caused by wood-destroying fungi, the most virulent of which is the *merulius lacrymans*, the true dry rot fungus. *Coniphora cerebella*, or cellar fungus as wet rot is sometimes called, is simpler to deal with, but it is important to be able to recognize the appearance and symptoms of both in order to eradicate them promptly.

The term 'dry rot' is misleading as it only occurs in damp timber. Since it usually starts in damp, unventilated corners that are hidden from view it may not be detected until it is well advanced. This is one of the main reasons why it should be looked for at the inspection stage. An unmistakable sign is cracking and bulging joinery, caused by the shrinkage of concealed timbers which have been attacked by the fungus. Suspected timbers can be tested by inserting the sharp point of a pen-knife gently into the wood. If dry rot is present the knife will meet with no resistance and the wood will crumble at its touch, but where the wood is healthy the tip of the knife will be gripped by the fibres, making it quite difficult to withdraw.

The dry rot fungus also has a characteristic smell, like toadstools, unmistakable where the air is stagnant. As the rot develops it produces millions of microscopic spores and silky threads which travel quickly over very large areas and spread more or less anywhere. If they fall on unprotected damp wood they will germinate and the whole process goes on repeating itself. Sometimes the fungus develops under floorboards and the spores will drift up through the cracks. They are easily blown about by air currents and will form a film of fine reddish-brown dust all over a room; this may well be one of the first visible signs of dry rot in a house.

The fungus will also penetrate brickwork and is capable of passing over inert substances such as stonework or metal or, in fact, almost any material in order to attack timber in the vicinity. It is possible, therefore, for dry rot to spread from cellar to attic, or from house to house, if it is not detected in time.

Wood under attack has a typical dark brown colour, is deeply cracked *across* the grain and is liable to split into small cubical pieces. It becomes parched and brittle, light in weight and inevitably loses its strength.

Wet rot, by contrast, refers to the decay of timber under very wet conditions. It often shows little or no visible signs of growth on the surface of the wood, though there may be considerable cracking *along* the grain. It is rather more insidious than dry rot in that it often causes internal rotting in floorboards or joists.

In all fungal attacks, ruthless eradication and repair are a matter of

A

B

Fig. 35   A. *Wet rot damage*
B. *Dry rot damage*

urgency, together with remedying the conditions which started the attack. It is necessary to know something about the architecture of the building when locating the cause of decay, for all rotten timber must be cut out and burnt on site, together with all shavings and sweepings, taking great care to prevent spore dispersal. When cutting out the decayed wood a safety margin of at least 2 feet beyond the bad portion is recommended. Infected plaster should also be cut out, with a safety margin of 1 foot round the bad area. Any walls showing signs of infection should be thoroughly scraped and sterilized (a blow lamp should be used with great care near dry timber) before being treated with an efficient fungicide. Any sound timber left in the vicinity should be liberally brushed or sprayed with a preservative, as should timber used for replacement if it has not already been treated at the timber yard. It is essential for all repairs to be carried out thoroughly if there is to be no reinfection.

This treatment is for wet and dry rot, but since wet rot is less virulent than dry rot it is not necessary to sterilize the brickwork in houses where it occurs. It can often be checked quite effectively by removing the source of dampness and rapidly drying the whole house.

The installation of a central heating system, combined with adequate ventilation, is the best method of preventing rot, for it will never occur in a sound dry house. In fact, with proper precautions there is no reason at all why old timber or a sound old building should ever be affected with this disease.

Timber pests   A recent survey indicated that as many as three houses in four have woodworm in a greater or lesser degree, and many old houses show unmistakable traces of it in their timbers even though it has long since been eliminated.

Woodworm is the grub or larva of the wood-destroying beetle. The beetle, red to blackish-brown in colour and from one tenth to one fifth of an inch long, lays eggs in the cracks and crevices of timber and furniture, and the grubs, when fully grown, bore into the timber, feeding upon it and filling galleries with the characteristic fine sand-like dust that often accumulates in little heaps beneath infested wood. When the grubs develop into beetles they bite their way out of the woodwork, leaving small round exit holes about one sixteenth of an inch in diameter, through which they fly. They emerge during spring and summer, when they crawl and fly about looking for suitable places in which to lay their eggs and so spread the area of infestation. They normally attack sapwood or softwoods, so heart of oak beams are immune from this particular pest.

They should be destroyed by a reliable insecticide applied from early spring to late summer, either brushed or sprayed on, as well as being injected into the flight holes to kill off any insects still in the timber. Where it is necessary to replace infested parts the new wood should be treated before it is used.

The *deathwatch beetle* is another pest which may be encountered in roof timbers. It gets its grim name from the fact that it makes a clicking sound which was formerly thought to presage death. The superstition has gone but the popular name clings with unnecessarily sinister implications. This beetle has a preference for hardwoods and those that are already in a state of decay are a favourite repository for the eggs. The insect is a dark mottled brown in colour, about a quarter to one third of an inch in length, larger than the common furniture beetle, and so leaves a larger exit hole, about one eighth of an inch in diameter. The presence of small pellets in the bore dust identify this beetle, but it is nevertheless advisable for the infected timbers to be inspected by a competent entomologist, if possible between April and June, which is the time when the beetles emerge. The surface dirt and bore dust should be scraped off the timbers before they are treated and a vacuum cleaner used to remove all debris. Then the appropriate insecticide should be brushed or sprayed on twice during the period April to June, and also injected into the holes. It is advisable to repeat this treatment for four consecutive years.

An architect or builder should be called in to check whether any timbers have been weakened sufficiently to need replacing, and reused wood, if showing the slightest damage, should be sterilized by heat or treated with insecticide. New oak heartwood does not normally need preservative treatment but, to be on the safe side, softwoods should be given at least a surface coating, or treated by one of the absorption processes.

The *house longhorn beetle* is brown or black in colour and one third of an inch in length, though the larvae may reach a length of $1\frac{1}{4}$ inches. Though it has been known on the Continent and South Africa, at present it is localized in this country and if its presence is suspected the householder is advised to call in the expert who will know how to exterminate it by the latest scientific means. Anyone who has a house in Surrey or Hampshire may possibly find this pest making its unwelcome appearance. It is insidious in that the larval period in England may be anything up to eleven years, during which time the damage caused inside a timber may leave it little more than a shell. There is very little external evidence of this beetle, except sometimes a slight unevenness of the wood over the borings.

All this information about timber pests may sound a good deal more alarming than it is in actual fact. It is simply a case of knowing one's enemy. Once known, there is a safe and certain remedy available for all cases of infestation.

Many people treat timbers with an insecticide during restoration purely as a precautionary measure, and there are a great number of preservation processes available today, all of which are equally effective. It remains for the householder to make his choice, according to his own particular needs. It is essential to remember that wherever poisonous vapours and chemicals are used, they must be handled with caution and kept well away from foodstuffs.

The British Wood Preserving Association, a scientific and professional body that sponsors research into the use of preservatives and fire retardants, offers a free advisory service on all problems connected with preservation and the fireproofing of timber. In addition, the leading manufacturers of proprietary brand insecticides and fungicides maintain advice bureaux where members of the public may seek expert advice or ask for a free test survey. They do a thoroughly professional job, under guarantee, of eradicating all forms of rot and pests.

Painting   Painting is the traditional way of protecting the exposed surfaces of softwood from moisture, abrasion and dirt, though certain very durable softwoods, such as Western red cedar, may be waterproofed by the use of a colourless liquid preparation, brushed on like paint, which will also help to preserve them. Apart from being a water repellent for timber, paint is also a preservative, for no insect will lay its eggs on the painted surface of wood.

For complete protection against moisture all the surfaces of the wood should be painted, particularly the end grain, which is most susceptible to damp. Careful preparation is the key to success, the basis of which is that the woodwork, particularly outside, should be clean and dry.

Wood that has not previously been painted should be rubbed or scraped down to remove dirt or grease, smoothed with sandpaper and dusted off before the application of a suitable primer. Any knots in the wood should be sealed with shellac knotting and rubbed down with abrasive paper when dry.

Previously painted wood that is generally in good condition should be washed down with soap and water or a detergent solution. Whilst wet, flatten the surface with an abrasive, then rinse off and allow to dry. Where it is not in good condition it should be cleaned off by scraping, removing all flaking paint in the process. For large surfaces a coarse sanding disc attached to an electric drill base is effective, but for smaller areas a good chemical stripper will suffice, using a broad stripping knife to scrape off the old paint to a smooth surface. All traces of the chemical should be washed off and the wood allowed to dry before work begins. Any bare timber must be primed before the new paint is put on. When the primer is quite hard, make good all cracks, nail holes or open joints with one of the proprietary filling compounds, after removing loose plaster from cracks with the point of a scraper. Large holes may be filled with wall plaster and smaller cracks with a cellulose filler, but cracks between two different surfaces, such as wood and plaster, should be filled with a multi-purpose filler. A great improvement can be effected by the careful filling of cracks. It will also eliminate a lot of the dust which can be a nuisance in old houses.

The kind of paint to be used will depend upon the conditions to which the finished work will be subjected. Full directions are usually supplied with each tin of paint, together with advice on the appropriate primer and undercoat to be used. In general, all the materials used in any one paint system should be obtained from the same manufacturer since they are specifically designed to be used together for the best results.

Exterior painting should not be carried out in bad weather conditions. Extremes of temperature can affect the setting and drying times and the finished appearance of the paint. Surface moisture from rain, fog, dew or condensation may reduce adhesion and also affect appearance. Neither should the completion of the painting process be too long delayed. Primers and undercoats, for instance, are not suitable for long periods of exposure.

Whether they are inside or outside, extra care should be taken with the painting of mouldings and other fine details, or the sharp outlines will be lost and something of the object of restoration will be defeated.

Owners of old timber-framed houses should also bear in mind that there are a number of fire-retardant paints and finishes which meet the requirements of the British Standards Institution. When exposed to fire they immediately form a dense insulating barrier which effectively resists the spread of flame and prevents the heat from penetrating the timber.

If any further advice is needed on this subject it may be obtained from one of the Building Centres or Home Improvement Centres. Detailed technical advice on any unusual or difficult problem may always be obtained from individual manufacturers, from the appropriate trade association, or from the Building Research Establishment.

White is the accepted colour for restoration paintwork and it is available now in a number of tones. Though weatherboarding is often seen stained or even tarred in some areas, it looks much better painted white.

There is no reason why colours should not be used in the interior, however – in the kitchen or the bathroom, for example, which will have been modernized, and for these areas, where steam is likely to accumulate, there are some good anti-condensation paints, which also check mould and fungus growths.

Painting ironwork has already been dealt with in Chapter 9. Properly carried out, this is the finest means of preserving all old ironwork, but the paint should always be black.

In all cases where it is normally used, the value of regular painting as a preservative measure cannot be overstressed.

Timber flooring   Old timber flooring should be preserved wherever possible, for there is no material to equal it for resilience and warmth. Some very old houses have wide floorboards which have a decided slope to them, and it would be a mistake to try to level them up. On the other hand, if an unequal surface is caused by an accumulation of dirt, sanding will help to remove this and bring the floor back to its proper level. Neglected parquet and wood-block floors can be resurfaced by rubbing the way of the grain with a fairly coarse steel wool, brushing off with a soft dusting brush as work proceeds. Old polish can be removed with turpentine substitute, but one should be careful to differentiate between dirty old polish and the patina of age, which will respond to wax polish and rubbing. Beeswax, where it can be obtained, serves both as a filler and sealer of the grain, but it needs a good deal of rubbing which many people are not prepared to give, particularly where a large surface is involved.

For a floor which is of no great importance from the 'antique' point of view, a sealer might be preferred, which will seal the pores of the wood and prevent the penetration of dust. There are many proprietary brands on the market that give excellent and long-lasting results, but the timber must always be properly prepared before they are applied. All other polishes and sealers must be removed with an abrasive cleaner, leaving a perfectly clean surface. A modern floor sealer does not normally require further treatment, but if an additional polish is preferred a resin emulsion should be used and not a paste wax polish which will make the surface far too slippery.

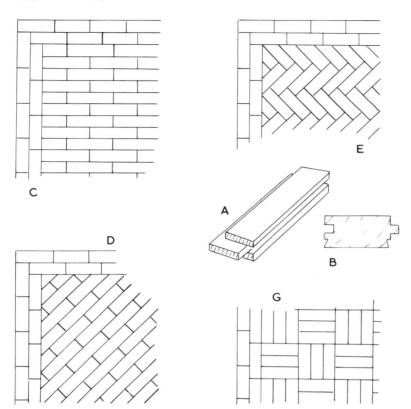

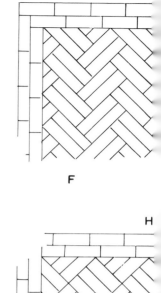

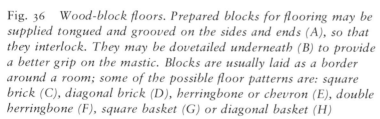

Fig. 36 *Wood-block floors. Prepared blocks for flooring may be supplied tongued and grooved on the sides and ends (A), so that they interlock. They may be dovetailed underneath (B) to provide a better grip on the mastic. Blocks are usually laid as a border around a room; some of the possible floor patterns are: square brick (C), diagonal brick (D), herringbone or chevron (E), double herringbone (F), square basket (G) or diagonal basket (H)*

Fig. 37 *Wood grain. As wood is a natural material, which will warp and shrink as its moisture content varies, the way a board is cut from the log controls its probable subsequent behaviour. A log is most simply converted to boards by cutting 'through-and-through' (A). A central board will then be cut radially and the lines of the annual rings will go across its end. It may get thinner as it dries, but it will remain flat (B). A board cut further out can be identified by the pattern of rings on its end and it may be*

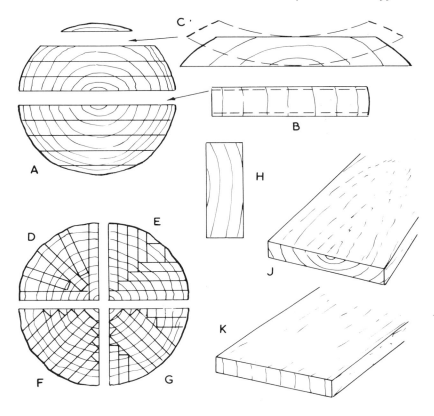

expected to warp (C). The probable behaviour of any board can
be considered as an attempt to straighten the annual rings on its
end. Cutting all boards radially (rift sawing) is wasteful (D).
Cutting a quarter section of the log alternate ways (E) produces
early boards truly radially-cut, and although others are
progressively further from radial, there is no waste. Other
methods of cutting (F and G) produce a greater number of rift-
sawn boards, but there is some waste. A beam or joist is better
with the annual rings vertical (H), if it is not rift-sawn. A
floorboard with a grain pattern on the surface, showing it was cut
across some way from the centre of the log (J), is liable to warp
and shrink. One with straighter lines, showing it was rift-sawn
(K), should remain flat and maintain its width. Figured or
wainscot oak is a board cut radially so as to slice through the
medullary rays which give the characteristic surface appearance

This preservative treatment makes floors not only easy to clean and resistant to wear but proof against pests. Timber floors that are properly cared for will mature with age and look good long after many synthetic materials have outlived their purpose.

Flagstones, brick and quarry tiles These old natural materials have their own qualities of texture and colour and the temptation to remove or cover them up should be resisted wherever it is practicable. They may be worn and uneven, hollow with the passage of footsteps of past generations, but this is part of their charm. If flagstones are positively dangerous in places, the levels can be adjusted by lifting and putting some weak mortar underneath. Worn bricks can be reversed. If they need repointing, mortar of a suitable colour should be used so that the general effect is not spoiled.

Quarry tiles that are dull and well-worn, with a patchy look about them, can be rejuvenated by a generous application of colourless wax, well rubbed in.

Ceramic tiles A householder who is fortunate to possess any old pottery tiles has something valuable and probably historic. Medieval tiles were mostly used for the floors of churches and monasteries, so one is not likely to come across those in ordinary houses; but there may well be some original patterned tiles or plain coloured tiles set in patterns on the floors of some Victorian and Edwardian houses. It was during the Victorian era and the crafts revival that took place at that time that the 'art potters' began to make decorative tiles for household use which were the delight of aesthetes. It was their hand-painted designs and styles that influenced the commercial manufacturers and some very beautiful items were produced at that time.

The Victorians adorned every suitable surface with tiles – the floors in the hall, the bathroom and the kitchen, on fireplace surrounds, on dados and even on furniture. Sometimes they were used singly, like a picture in a frame, or a series made up a pattern in the form of a mural. They were all delightfully attractive, with highly glazed surfaces, easy to keep clean. It is difficult to understand the mentality of the people who, during the early part of this century, swept away these decorative Victorian tiles and substituted ugly plain slab ones. They ripped them from floors, walls and fireplaces alike, with no regard for their fine artistic merit. When old buildings were demolished, the tiles were broken or lost, but hopefully, when some demolition is going on today, some of these tiles can still be salvaged and used for restoration work. Another hunting ground for the restorer is the ubiquitous market stall or a jumble sale. There are occasional bargains to be picked up in this way.

Old tiles can be restored by H. & R. Johnson Ltd, who revived the old firm of Maw's Picture Tiles. They also make perfect replicas of old designs, using the age-old method of tube-lining and hand painting.

More important still is the encaustic floor tile revival undertaken by this firm during the last decade or so, a very welcome contribution to architectural conservation in general. Some of these floorings are unique, having their roots in medieval design, and deserve to be preserved. Now, thanks to successful research into original methods by specialist craftsmen, it is possible for worn or damaged tiles to be repaired or replaced in their entirety. Restoration, in this sense, is eminently worthwhile.

Laying tiles There must be an even surface before any wall or floor covering can be laid.

Concrete floors should be covered with a screeding compound which is left to dry to a smooth, level finish. Unglazed or ceramic tiles can be laid on this foundation. Ceramic tiles can also be laid on a timber floor if the joints are strong enough to take the extra weight. If they are, a metal mesh should be laid first and then a layer of screeding compound brushed over the top.

Attention to details such as these, and many others, is part of the overall preservation of old buildings, which provide the right settings for most natural materials. Where these are preserved and used again they will form an important part of the whole and help the old house to live again in its own benign atmosphere.

11

Conversions

'Ripe for conversion' is the favourite jargon of estate agents wishing to sell derelict property, but what exactly does the term convey? As I see it, conversion covers a wide area, taking in all kinds of buildings that have outlived their original purpose but are still serviceable. They may include anything from an old mill to a disused church, as well as the more conventional farmhouses and cottages. With a little imagination and a lot of hard work they can be converted into homes that are completely individual, if not unique.

The Pump House   For example, few people would look at a building so essentially utilitarian as an old pump house and see in it an attractive family house, but an architect with ingenuity and vision did just this.

When I saw it this building was already converted, prior to being put up for sale, so the work was not done to individual requirements in this instance. Nevertheless, it is a house that anyone would be proud to own, planned as it is to get the maximum benefit from the original old stone building. The actual pump house has been restored, with the stonework looking as good as new, and made into one large, lofty, dignified living room, with the original arches and high circular window retained. Had it been carved up to make more rooms it would have belittled its importance. As it is, the architect built on an extension, using matching materials, so that the one flows smoothly from the other to give the necessary living space. As seen on the plan (Fig. 38), there is ample accommodation with four bedrooms and two bathrooms, and plenty of well-fitted cupboards and fitments in the kitchen.

The extension has a mansard roof, slated to match the original pump house and hung with slate tiles at the gable end. The mansard roof is a design which has two slopes each side, the lower being steeper than the upper, thus providing more space for rooms than would be obtained with a normal roof of single slope, and in this case Velux roof lights are used to good effect, with storage space built in

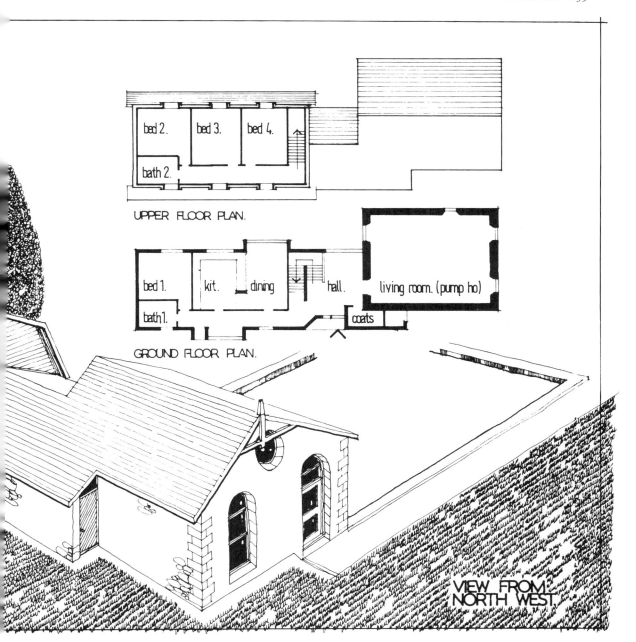

bed 2.

bed 3.

bed 4.

bath 2.

UPPER FLOOR PLAN.

bed 1.

kit.

dining

hall.

living room. (pump ho)

bath 1.

coats

GROUND FLOOR PLAN.

VIEW FROM NORTH WEST.

Fig. 38 *Plan of The Pump House, Helensburgh, Dunbartonshire*

beneath them. In the garden the old water wheel has been left as a feature, a permanent reminder of the old days when the pump house supplied the water for the town of Helensburgh before it grew to its present size. It served its purpose then, as it serves its purpose now, albeit in a decorative capacity.

Apart from the fact that many discarded old buildings can usually be bought for the proverbial song, the people who buy them are individuals who bring their own kind of genius to bear on the problems of conversion. But, speaking generally, it would be a mistake for anyone to embark on extensive alterations without having some knowledge of the original structure, so that it can be adapted without taking away any of its essential simplicity and character.

Some houses, however, are far from being simple, but they still have a definite value when it comes to the question of conversion for modern living. Certain Victorian houses come into this category.

Flats   Victorian architecture was sometimes ornate – it has been called 'romantic' – with a curious mixture of past styles and their embellishments which the owners thought would lend importance and dignity to their homes. The popularity of the Gothic style is evidenced today in the many houses of this period that survive. They were built in more spacious days, when there were servants in plenty to inhabit the great basements and attics, and their rooms are large and lofty, with big sash windows and wooden shutters to close at night, and nearly always a tower which was considered essential. Splendid, solid old houses, but no longer practical as one-family homes; however, because their structure is so sound, they make excellent modern flats.

There is a particularly good example of this kind of conversion at Grosvenor Hill, Wimbledon, in south-west London, where a tall, Gothic-style house, plus a stable at the side, is now four spacious self-contained flats. The house is typical of its age, with a steeply pitched slate roof and doors and windows with pointed arches, and inside are some eighteen to twenty rooms on four floors.

This conversion has been carried out to conservation standards, which means that the exterior is as the original (Plate 36). Only the interior, which unfortunately was badly damaged by squatters and vandals during the years when the building stood derelict, has been completely refurbished and modernized, while keeping as many of the original features as possible. Each flat has two bedrooms, a sitting

36   *A Victorian Gothic house in Wimbledon, London, converted into four flats. All the old period features have been retained on the exterior. The interior is modernized*

room, a fitted kitchen, a bathroom and a second w.c. as well as plenty of cupboard space.

The building is brick, old yellow London stocks, with some interesting details around the doors and windows. It was all so grimy that it had to be cleaned by acid spray and the brickwork repointed to bring it back to its original appearance. Some plain moulded barge boards trimming the gables were reinstated, but some of the old patterned ones were too rotten to replace, and would have been too costly to have had made in replica.

The roof was virtually taken apart to make sure all the rafters were sound and free from woodworm, then it was entirely reslated, using most of the original slates and matching up with similar ones from a demolished building of the same period where necessary. A lot of shoring up and propping up went on at this stage, but in the end the structure was pronounced thoroughly sound.

Several of the windows had been badly damaged by vandals, but they were such a characteristic feature of the old house that they were restored down to the last detail. New woodwork was slotted in, moulded to the Victorian pattern in the builder's own workshop. There were many rough, gaping nail-holes where the timbers had received harsh treatment, and these were made good with plastic padding which is quite unnoticeable under the new white paint.

The floorboards in the basement were rotten, and had to be pulled out and destroyed. They were replaced with a solid concrete floor and at the same time a damp-proof course was inserted by the injection method.

In the main rooms some carved plaster moulding was made good for ogee-type architraves, but sadly the original moulded plaster ceiling roses and cornices had been wantonly destroyed. Some of the cornices were replaced with moulded coving, the plasterer erecting it on site, but the ceilings wait for some enterprising tenants to reinstate the period plasterwork.

It was not possible to keep the open fireplaces as such, because the 'gathering' of the flues would have made their use impractical, but there is a splendid Victorian metal chimneypiece in the first-floor sitting room which makes a good focal point. All the flats now have independent central heating.

The house was not altered structurally and has kept its Victorian Gothic appearance in every particular, which has earned the approval of the planning authorities; all the more so, because there are now four homes in place of one, and all achieved without spoiling the traditional character of this little corner of Wimbledon village.

Cottages The Victorians who had country estates of any size often built very good servants' quarters, of good solid construction and fair-sized rooms. They can have had no idea how we, in this 'welfare' age, would snap them up for conversion into modern homes!

Making two or more old cottages into a more commodious single one has now become fairly common practice, and where the basic construction is sound it is a worthwhile proposition. Time and again one sees the not-so-humble cottage in the country which is in reality two parts merged into one to make a convenient modern residence.

The conversion is usually quite simple, giving the owner a flexibility in planning to make as many or as few rooms as he needs. I have seen a row of five cottages made into one house in this way, producing a smooth flowing unity which is very restful to the eye and easy to live in.

To take an example: two cottages at Cardross, Scotland, once the coachman's and the gardener's on a big estate, escaped demolition

37   Kilmahew, Dunbartonshire, before conversion, originally two small Victorian cottages

when they were sold to a couple who saw in them the kind of family home they could create from them. There was also space enough to build on an extension for elderly parents. The situation was ideal.

They were typical early Victorian cottages, with small rooms, no damp-proof course and few conveniences, but the structure was sound, with stone walls 2 feet thick and a fine slate roof – a good enough basis on which to start work.

Planning permission was obtained for some structural alterations for which plans were submitted by an architect, and a grant was forthcoming towards the installation of a large septic tank to supply both cottage and extension. Also, a silicone-injected damp-proof course was put in by a specialist firm. The basic essentials thus catered for, the two cottages were then redesigned to make one, without spoiling their Victorian character.

The ground floor of the first cottage originally comprised three very small rooms, one of which formed the entrance with a steep staircase leading off it. It was relatively simple to remove the non-loadbearing

Fig. 39 *The sitting room at Kilmahew, during conversion. The boards are against the site of the old staircase*

dividing walls to open up one good-size sitting room, which, with the high ceiling, looks far more in proportion than did the previous 'bitty' layout. The old staircase was removed, new joists put in, the ceiling and floor made good and the wall bricked up. The remaining small room at the back now makes an excellent study, with a new window fitted in the external wall and new doors to a deep cupboard. The cupboard was strapped with 2 × 1-inch treated framing and lined with foil-backed plasterboard. The floor, which was originally concrete flags, had a new damp-proof membrane put down and new concrete laid on the flags.

A door from the sitting room gives access to the second cottage which had two rooms on the ground floor. A new kitchen was formed here which now contains an oil-fired central heating boiler in place of the old fireplace. Its position in the middle of the house means that it diffuses warmth to every part and so saves energy. The kitchen fittings are well planned and labour-saving to the last degree. They include ample work tops, a breakfast bar with storage cupboards beneath, a dry goods store and a ventilated larder.

A new doorway between the kitchen and the adjoining playroom, or living room, was opened up and a new window made through the external wall. This is a fine room for the family, with the open fireplace put to good use to make it cosy and cheerful at all times.

At the back of this room the old Victorian kitchen and bathroom were made into a modern utility room with a small shower room and toilet attached – useful after a spell of gardening. Here the timber floor had to be lifted and a new concrete one laid on a damp-proof membrane. It is all very compact, with room to keep garden boots and coats stowed away neatly.

The original stairway in the second cottage has been kept intact and is now the only means of access to the upper floor. Here there are four bedrooms, so that the three children each have their own domain. A bathroom was formed between the bedrooms and a new cupboard was built to enclose the hot-water tank. All this was achieved by taking down the cross walls and making a narrow landing with a new timber stud and plasterboard partition. The plasterboard was of double thickness, insulated between the glass-fibre rolls to make it soundproof. This gives each bedroom its separate door, but since it also blocked out light, Velux roof lights were fitted in each room, which supplied the need very well.

Some of the ceilings had to be replastered and there was a moment of panic when it was discovered that some joists above the kitchen had been burnt and had to be replaced without delay.

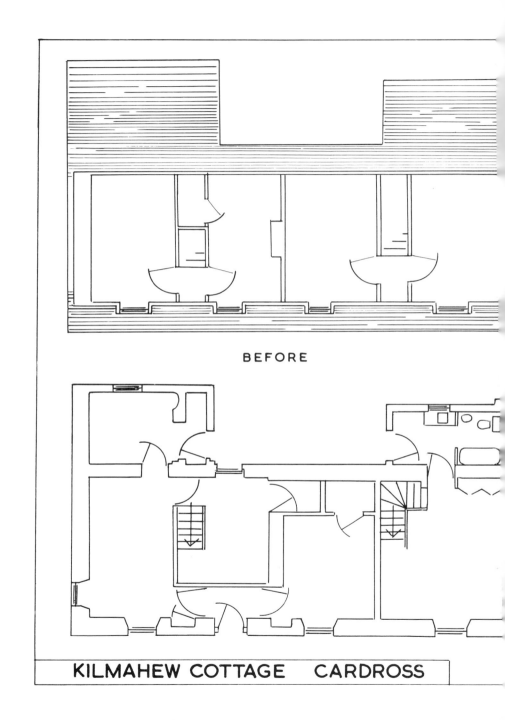

BEFORE

KILMAHEW COTTAGE   CARDROSS

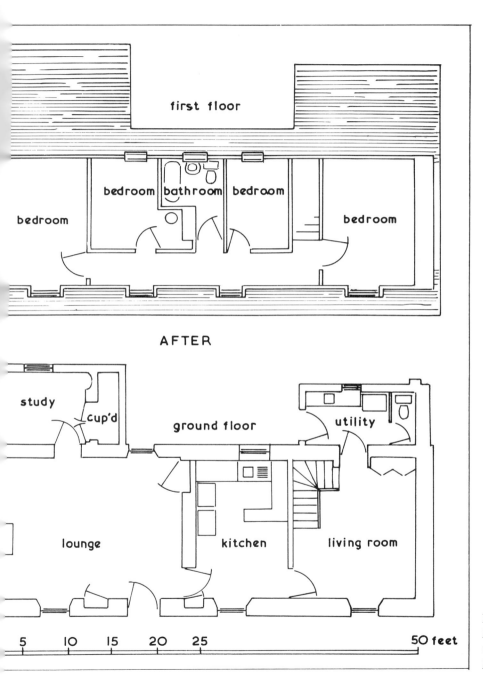

first floor

bedroom | bedroom | bathroom | bedroom

bedroom

AFTER

study

cup'd

ground floor

utility

lounge

kitchen

living room

5   10   15   20   25   50 feet

Fig. 40 *Plan of Kilmahew Cottage, Cardross, Dunbartonshire*

All this stripping down of ceilings and walls, irksome at the time, gave the owners the satisfaction of confirming that the structure was sound and they now feel comfortable for many years to come.

The original double hung sash windows were kept intact but because of the prevalence of high winds and rain in this part of the country they were sealed at the bottom to keep out rain and double glazed on the ground floor. Eventually the windows on the upper floors will also be done, when funds permit.

The exterior was refurbished by rendering with two skins of cement and dashed with pebbles for further weatherproofing. A porch was built out and a new front door built on to the west side of it to give shelter from the cold winds. The roof was of good sturdy Ballachulish slates and relatively few needed renewing when the roof lights were put in. The replacements were obtained from a demolished building and supplied by a scrap merchant at very low cost; they match the original slates exactly.

38   *Kilmahew, after conversion. The porch was built out with an entrance door on the west side, where it is more sheltered. A garage has been built on at the side, and the garden is beautifully landscaped*

39 *The new sitting room at Kilmahew, with the original double hung sash windows restored. The fireplace is characteristically Victorian, with a cast-iron interior and Dutch tiled reveals*

The interior of the house shows the same meticulous attention to detail and care in planning. In the large sitting room the old floor was taken up and then relaid with oak parquet tiles on chipboard insulated with glass fibre. A large carpet thrown on this still leaves enough of the polished surround to give a good background for furniture.

To keep the Victorian character a search began for the right mouldings for skirting boards and architraves round the doors, and a cornice of moulded polyurethane, bought in lengths, looks exactly like plaster as it would have been in those early days. The old Victorian fireplace with its cast-iron interior and Dutch-tiled reveals was restored, though one or two of the tiles were missing. Another search resulted in suitable replacements and the fire still burns brightly, after all these years. A William Morris design wallpaper completes the picture of a charming Victorian family room.

The porch is just as well conceived, giving plenty of room to walk in and close the door on the elements. It has a floor of Italian ceramic tiles and a window hung with curtains of old hand-made Victorian lace which gives the right initial impression of what the rest of the house will be like.

So that they could get the final details correct the owners drew a ground plan on paper and cut out pieces of paper to scale representing furniture and fitments. This way they made sure that no space was wasted and everything fitted in beforehand. It is an idea worth considering since it saves so much disappointment and wasted effort should some things prove to be in the wrong place.

With the exception of a very few specialized jobs the owners did all the work themselves while living in the house with their three children. It was undoubtedly very hard work but they could not have got the house they wanted in any other way. Now they have the satisfaction of bringing up their children in the country they love as well as caring for elderly parents in the extension they were able to have built on as an integral part of the house.

As they were the first people to own the house, apart from the estate, they had to have title deeds created, which makes Kilmahew Cottage a house in its own right. It is a far cry from the nondescript old gardener's and coachman's cottages it once was, which is yet another proof of how an old, out-of-date building can be adapted to live a long and useful life in this modern age.

Drumglas   Farmhouses, as a rule, lend themselves to conversion more readily than most houses. They have disused dairies, vast kitchens and various outhouses that present endless possibilities to the present-day planner and leave room for manoeuvre in many directions.

This was borne out in a house I came across near Gartocharn in Dunbartonshire, called Drumglas. Originally it had been a single-storey stone building, long and low, built to an L shape, as seen on the original composite photograph (Plate 40). It was a typical single-span building, a development of the 'long house' with rooms going right across from side to side and entered one from the other. In its early days it was probably what was known as a two-parlour house, with the addition of a byre or a stable at one end as an integral part of the plan. When the present owners took it the porch opened into a corridor connecting with a living room on one side, a dining room on the other and a bedroom in between, accessible from the dining room. Part of the bedroom had been used to accommodate a staircase situated in the corridor and this led up to a landing with two attic bedrooms, one each side of it, with small roof lights as the only means of light and ventilation. A small kitchen extension had been built on at the back.

It had great possibilities for a man who wanted to combine farming with other business activities, making a home for his family at the same time. He took a wise decision in consulting an architect who is as well known for his sensitivity to the environment as for his skill in restoring old buildings. Together they worked out a plan to suit both

40 *Drumglas, near Gartocharn, Dunbartonshire, before conversion*

husband and wife, and although this involved some necessary structural work it has not altered the exterior of the old farmhouse to any great extent. It has, instead, enhanced it.

As seen on the plan (Fig. 41) the roof was raised on one wing to make two rooms on the first floor, and a new entrance was made from a rather imposing-looking portico salvaged from a demolished pub in Glasgow. The original entrance was blocked up but all the original windows on the front elevation facing the courtyard have been retained, or replaced in replica, so that the frontage is symmetrical, and the stone walls have been whitewashed.

The original roof was slate, of no particular merit, with some parts in corrugated asbestos, so it was decided to reroof the entire building with Marley Modren grey concrete tiles, which merge in with the landscape very effectively.

The old byre in the south-east wing occupied considerable space but this was successfully converted to make an entrance hall which leads on to a kitchen at one side and a large family room at the other. In addition, a bathroom was built into the back part of the hall.

41   *The new drawing room at Drumglas. The head of the open staircase is seen in the background (left). The wide modern windows give superb views over Loch Lomond*

Fig. 41   *Plan of Drumglas, near Gartocharn, Dunbartonshire*

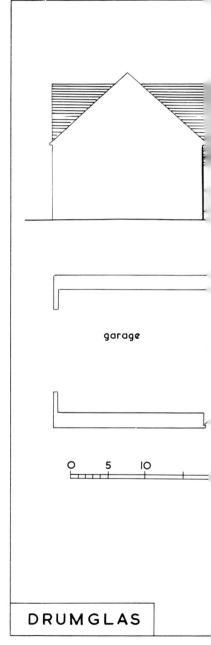

garage

O   5   10

DRUMGLAS

An open Oregon pine staircase leads up to the first floor and the pleasant, quiet drawing room that took shape there. Here the architect allowed himself some latitude and made wide picture windows in the back wall to take full advantage of the magnificent views over Loch Lomond. Built-in window seats are both charming and practical here, providing extra seating when it is needed. To add to the air of solid comfort an open fireplace was built into the wall between the windows, with a chimney provided for it in the outer wall. The new floorboards are pine, sealed and polished and well sprung, for this room is well used at all times. It is indeed a gracious room, far removed from the old concept of a workaday farmhouse.

The only space left to put a guest room was at the end of this room, but since it has its own toilet accommodation it is quite self-contained and conveniently removed from the everyday activities of the house; and guests, of course, enthuse about the views.

Downstairs, the remainder of the original one-storey building has been well planned to take a master bedroom and a boys' bedroom, with a corridor connecting the two. A second bathroom slots in well

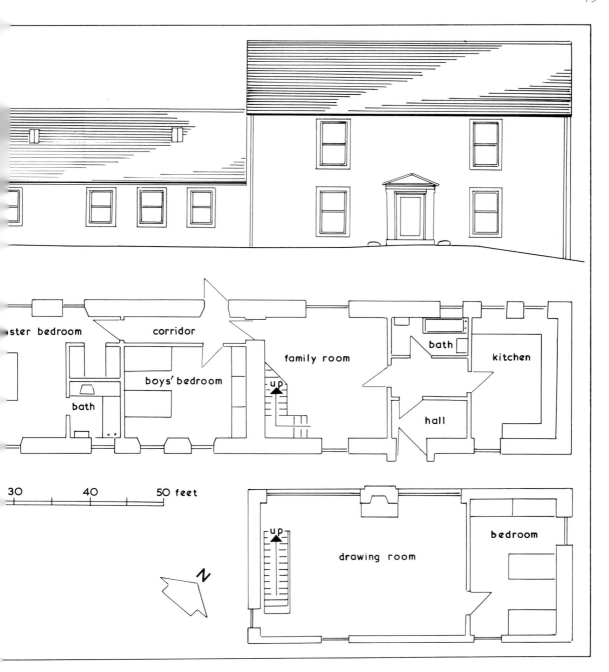

ster bedroom   corridor

family room

bath

kitchen

boys' bedroom

up

hall

bath

30   40   50 feet

up

bedroom

drawing room

N

between the two bedrooms and there is still space beyond all these rooms for a very large garage.

There was also a fairly vast space to fill in between this end of the house and a byre and this has been transformed into a splendid games room, complete with swimming pool and everything that is needed to entertain guests. It seems to give the final touch to this delightful family home.

The south-west wing is still mainly occupied with farm buildings, but the old granary, which was very lofty and spacious, has been ceiled in to make two floors, the upper one of which makes a very large and useful office, still leaving plenty of storage space below. The roof has been left with its open rafters and looks much more interesting than if it had been plastered in.

42   Drumglas, after conversion, with the roof raised on one wing to make two rooms on the first floor

Seeing Drumglas farmhouse now, set in its sweeping courtyard against a backdrop of magnificent Scottish scenery, one finds it hard to believe that all this was achieved on a very tight budget and that the owners endured a considerable amount of cold and discomfort by living in one of the barns until they were compelled by weather conditions to move into the house, camping in one of the rooms as work proceeded. But, they said, it was worth it to get what they wanted, for no new home could compare with this.

Peniel Chapel   It is a sad reflection on our times that so many of our old churches and chapels are disused for lack of support, but probably the next best use to which those of manageable size can be put is to convert them into homes. This is usually very successful for they are spacious, airy buildings, lending themselves to individual planning very well indeed. They also contain many interesting period features that can often be built into the general design.

43   Peniel Chapel, Newtown, Powys, after conversion. An original Gothic window over the porch was retained. The schoolroom at the side awaits conversion (Don Griffiths)

This was so with Peniel Chapel, near Newtown, Powys. It was the outcome of the great religious revival of 1859 and it is interesting to note that it was built for the cost of about £300 and opened in 1862 for the purpose of worship. The plot of land was generously given by Lord Sudeley, so the outlay was for the building only, no doubt a princely sum in those days. A schoolroom was added at the rear after the completion of the original building and this was sold, with the chapel, to a private owner in 1979. He employed a local specialist builder to draw up plans and redesign the interior and this has been done with great expertise and regard for the original materials.

The building itself was a simple one, of no great architectural merit, but its structure was sound and had been well cared for by the chapel authorities. It was built of brick which had been roughcast on the external walls at some time, with a natural Welsh slate roof and high Gothic windows, typical of its period. The main attraction of the interior was in the wealth of pitch pine joinery of high quality, and a very fine coffered-effect ceiling which offered great possibilities when the new house was visualized.

Fig. 42 shows the original building, comprising the body of the

Fig. 42 *Peniel Chapel, before conversion*

chapel with two aisles and a central, raised pulpit with steps leading up to it from each side. At the back of the pulpit a door led into the schoolroom, which had a kitchen leading off it, and there was also the usual toilet accommodation. Now, a new main entrance has been made into the schoolroom at the side and the old entrance is a window. The lofty schoolroom has been made into a fine living room, left at full height with a gallery over it at one end. Part of it, however, had to be ceiled in, to take the second bedroom on the first floor, leaving the exposed joists as a feature. The old kitchen was converted into a hallway with a porch built on to the side of it. At one side is a staircase leading to the first floor, at the other a shower room and cloakrooms. Beyond this an extension has been built for a double garage. A door at the back of the hall leads into the new kitchen which, in turn, leads into the dining room and the living room. A door from the kitchen leads into two workshops which are thus accessible from the house. It is all a very ingenious use of space and very well planned.

Making another floor brought its problems, for the floor of the new kitchen had to be lowered by digging out to a depth of about 3 feet in order to raise the height of the ceiling. This gave the opportunity of making the floor completely damp-proof by laying hard core on earth, then a layer of solid concrete topped by joists on which pine boards were laid. With new units in place, it is now a very attractive and serviceable kitchen.

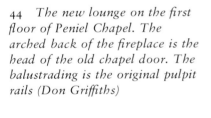

44   *The new lounge on the first floor of Peniel Chapel. The arched back of the fireplace is the head of the old chapel door. The balustrading is the original pulpit rails (Don Griffiths)*

The first floor has a large lounge, accessible by a staircase from the dining room below. Its main feature is a wide, open fireplace which takes advantage of an existing chimney. Its mantelshelf is part of the trefoil-patterned dado which was once round the chapel walls, and the arched back to the log store is the head of the old chapel door.

At the back of the lounge is the main bedroom, with a bathroom attached, and at the other side is the gallery overlooking the living room. The purpose of this gallery – apart from its considerable decorative aspect – is to give access to a second bedroom at one end and a third bedroom and second bathroom at the other end. A small landing and a staircase lead to the hallway below, which is a very convenient arrangement.

The schoolroom, or living room, had still to be finished when I saw it but the design had been worked out. Overall, it is an excellent conversion, making the best possible use of every inch of space, even to making an accessible and sizeable loft over the garage. Best of all, the fine old pitch pine has been reused, some of it as stair and gallery balustrades and some being put aside for further use later on. Part of the pulpit has been used to make a cabinet in the lounge and there are many other features in the house where the old joinery is in evidence.

It is a pity from the aesthetic point of view that the original Gothic windows on the front elevation were discarded in favour of modern windows, which tend to throw the building out of scale, but the making of two storeys no doubt presented its problems. A small

Fig. 43   *An artist's impression of the new schoolroom/sitting room at Peniel Chapel, showing the gallery*

Gothic window has been retained over the porch, however, to remind us of the house's origins; the little chapel lives again in a new guise.

Loft conversions   Conversion can also mean converting a loft or an attic into a room fit to be used. This is no new idea, for 'raising the roof' seems to have been practised by some house owners way back in Tudor times. I came across an ancient timber-framed wattle and daub house at Castle Caereinion, Powys, which had had the eaves raised at some time in the past (the present owner did not know when) and a window inserted in the gable, thus greatly improving the height of the bedrooms (Plate 45). It was obviously part of the restoration of a former age as the timbers are so weathered that they look as if they have always been there. The fact that they have been added to the original structure enhances the charm and character of the house rather than mars it.

Some other old houses in the Welsh border counties have adopted this method, which does not detract from the look of a building in any

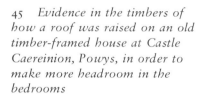

45   Evidence in the timbers of how a roof was raised on an old timber-framed house at Castle Caereinion, Powys, in order to make more headroom in the bedrooms

way, while making it altogether more convenient to live in. It is an idea worth noting, but those who wish to do the same thing nowadays should first make sure that restrictions do not forbid the raising of the roof line. While work of this nature is going on there is another opportunity for a close inspection of the roof spaces for rot, which is likely to occur anywhere where dampness, stagnant air and warmth are combined.

I saw an up-to-date version of this idea of building upwards at Kilcreggan, in Scotland. It was in fact an extension built over a large garage, the original walls of which were so stout that it was possible to build a wood-framed second floor over it. The entrance is at the back of the garage, with a staircase built up to the new floor which is virtually contained within a mansard roof. The walls are squared off and Velux roof windows are set within deep splays so that the space beneath them can take built-in chests for storage purposes. It is a spacious, pleasant room, admirably suited to its role as a games room

46   A wood-framed extension built over a garage at Kilcreggan, Strathclyde, with a utility room at the side

47 *The spacious games room over the garage at Kilcreggan. The mansard roof allows cupboard space under the wide window sills. Cupboards are also built into the slanting splays at the sides*

and studio combined, for with a further large, wide window at the end, the lighting is excellent. It also gives access to a separate utility room with further valuable storage space and, in addition, the whole extension is self-contained with its own water heating so that it is independent of the house. All this extra space was badly needed to enable children to play freely and also to allow a busy furniture designer to work and store equipment. Although the architect Andrew G. Black designed it, most of the work was done by the owners themselves, who are delighted with the result.

It is further proof of how most problems can be overcome where there is a will to do so. The beauty of this extension is the way in which it fits so snugly into the hilly countryside, seeming to form part of the background, for there is nothing disruptive about it.

The roof is of slate, with slate-hanging on the sides of the mansard, although these are in fact asbestos tiles, to reduce costs. They are such a good substitute that they deceive the eye at first sight and they blend in perfectly with the slate roofing of the old house which is in close proximity.

So, while roof extensions are no new thing, the modern method of building them is right up to date. They fit into any old house provided it has a pitched roof covered with conventional building materials and there is adequate standing room in it. In fact, the steeper the pitch of the roof the more space there will be to get under it and it also gives a better water run-off.

It is worth spending a considerable amount of time at the planning stage making sure you achieve precisely what you want, in keeping with the house and its setting. Basically, it is a question of improving on a room that is already there – an attic or a loft – and this kind of conversion is a very popular way of using the wasted space contained within a pitched roof. Also, by improving on the existing structure of the house it adds to the value of the property.

These extra rooms can be used as a sewing room, a studio, a study (it can be peaceful away from the main activities of the house), a games room, an extra bathroom, or what you will. The possibilities are endless and the very shape and structure of a room in the roof results in something with a lot of character.

It is advisable to get an architect's opinion on the structural design, or to employ a reliable builder. Be wary of the mushroom firms who inevitably try to cash in on a popular idea.

First, you will need advice about establishing access that is suitable to your particular conversion. You can have a permanently fixed staircase which can be a straight flight, or a staircase with quarter landings which saves on space. Or you can have a spiral staircase or a purpose-made retractable ladder. The latter is regarded as a movable fitting and does not need to comply with building regulations. The best place for a fixed staircase is usually above the stairwell, but make sure that it matches the existing one if it is to follow over it. A spiral staircase may take up less room, but it has to be negotiated with great care and is therefore not suitable where there are elderly people or children about. Also, it may look out of place in your type of house. Loft ladders come in various designs and you should look closely at the manufacturer's specifications before making a choice.

The next most important point is the method of construction of the floor of the loft. It is possible to strengthen the floor simply by bolting extra joists to the existing ones to take the extra load. Though it is quite legal to do this, it is not very satisfactory since the load is then distributed unevenly and can result in the ceilings beneath cracking and falling. By far the most satisfactory solution is to construct a completely separate floor, suspending it from the outside walls (or inside wall where it is feasible).

The new room also needs proper heating and insulation to stabilize the temperature all the year round. The walls can be insulated with a glass-fibre blanket or polystyrene board, and similar materials should be laid under the new floor. If it is intended to use electric heating appliances it is a simple job to fit power points in suitable places at the same time as you are wiring for lighting, but if you want to extend the central heating system into the attic area, first check that your boiler has capacity for the additional output. If you have to move the existing water tank this is the time to consider what water supply, if any, you would like in the new extension. Bear in mind that any new gas installations should be referred to your local gas board. With a little care and forethought you can make the room warm in winter and cool in summer, as well as being properly ventilated all the year round.

Most loft conversions have a dormer window, which can provide only a restricted amount of light. This type of window often requires considerable rebuilding of the roof and may not always be ideal for a traditional house. It is probably best to have Velux roof windows, which can be positioned exactly where light is required or to take advantage of a view, and they do not disrupt the line of the roof.

The main aim at all times should be to make the whole conversion look as if it is part of the original house and this should not be too difficult. In some cases planning permission may not be necessary, as it may come within the 'permitted development' rule. Nevertheless, it is always wise to check with the local planning officer and to try to get his agreement in writing that planning permission is not required. If planning permission is needed he will advise you on the correct procedures and let you know what is or is not likely to be acceptable to your particular planning authority.

12

Modernization and Interior Decoration

Living in an old house need not mean forgoing all modern comforts. There is no reason at all to go back to the days of poor sanitation, inconvenient kitchens, inadequate bathrooms and an ice-cold house. Not even the hardiest enthusiast would want to live in the past to that extent and there is little virtue in doing so these days, for times have changed and our outlook and mode of living have changed with them.

One of the greatest joys of living in an old house of any period is that there is usually room for manoeuvre, and modern amenities like central heating, labour-saving kitchen quarters and up-to-date plumbing can easily be incorporated into the building during the initial upheaval of reconditioning. This way one has time to consider the positioning of the apparatus, seeing that it is done discreetly so that it merges into the general background. Where any structural alteration is involved it goes without saying that this requires the advice of an architect or qualified builder in the first place.

The electrical system   The most urgent requirement will probably be to check the electrical installations. If these are faulty they may well be dangerous or even lethal. It is a known fact that, next to arson, electricity is the cause of nearly all fires in the United Kingdom and many a valuable old property has gone up in flames as the result of a faulty electrical circuit.

Any house over twenty-five years old is very likely to have been wired with rubber-covered cables which can deteriorate and possibly disintegrate, leaving the bare copper conductors exposed. Many of our older properties have an electrical installation designed for the days when there were very few appliances in daily use, and consequently we now have a situation where systems are often overloaded and are a source of potential risk. Usually the old electrical system incorporates the old-style fuse box with rewirable fuses. These are now replaced by fuse boards, some of which contain miniature circuit breakers – abuse-proof and convenient to use.

Obviously, if your house needs a complete new wiring system it should be handled in a professional manner and it is best to use a member of the Electrical Contractors' Association, which guarantees all members' work. This is one of the areas where it does not do to try to cut costs.

The owner of a timber-framed house should remember that oak contains tannic acid, which has a corrosive action on lead; lead-covered cable should never be fixed to oak beams because of fire risk.

When rewiring is being undertaken make provision for plenty of outlets for appliances. It is always useful to have plugs handy and it eliminates the risk of accidents from trailing flexes and overloaded sockets. The use of adaptors should be avoided for this reason. Sockets at counter height rather than on the skirting board in the kitchen might be considered. They are far more convenient when using an electric iron or a kettle, for instance.

Where wall and floor insulation is being put in it is a good idea to incorporate the general wiring with it to save pulling the house about unnecessarily. Also, the system should be designed and installed before colour schemes are planned and before floor coverings are put down.

Central heating　This comes high up on the list of modernization projects and few people would wish to be without it these days. Though it is expensive to install in the first place it is a wise investment, as it increases the value of a house and benefits it by keeping it dry and warm. Also, plumbing is better protected, reducing the danger of frozen pipes in winter virtually to zero. It need not be expensive to run if it is correctly controlled and programmed.

The householder has a good choice of fuels – solid fuel, gas, oil or electricity – as well as different types of central heating systems, i.e. 'wet' (hot-water pipes and radiators) or 'dry' (warm air flowing through ducts), but the system chosen will largely be determined by the type of house and the area in which it is situated. It is therefore advisable to seek expert advice in the first place to make sure that the preferred system can be efficiently controlled. Free advice is obtainable from the larger electricity or gas showrooms, or by contacting the Building Centre in London or a local building centre.

For a small house or cottage it may be an advantage to have electric storage heaters, providing this service is laid on. There is little or no structural disturbance involved in their fitting and consequently no mess. Off-peak storage heaters can be fitted at any time, after the decorating is done, so that their size, position and colouring can be chosen at leisure to blend in with the overall house plan.

The ducted warm-air system can be run by either electricity or gas and is installed by embedding the ducts in a solid concrete floor and allowing the heated air to escape through grilles placed where they are needed. If this method is chosen it is best installed when a new floor is being laid. Its great advantages are that it warms the house uniformly, it is clean and there are no visible appliances to take up space in a room.

A radiator heating system can also be fixed quite unobtrusively and need not mar the appearance of an old house, especially if slender-type radiators are chosen and they are painted to match the wall behind them. They should not affect the character of their surroundings. Any piping which has to pass through walls should be fixed with as little disruption to woodwork or masonry as possible. Wherever it is practicable the run of the pipes should be kept away from old oak, lest the dry heat causes the timber to warp and break its joints.

Air is called dry when it holds very much less than its total moisture capacity; put in simple terms, when we heat up the air it will take moisture from wherever it can get it, from all surrounding surfaces. Moisture lost from wood surfaces makes furniture, especially antiques and old panelling, warp and crack. Glues dry out, causing joints to loosen and veneers to lift off, and it is as well to bear this in mind when placing radiators. There is, however, a remedy for all these problems and that is in the installation of humidifiers which will add moisture to the air. There are various kinds available today, cheap to buy and easy to use. The most convenient kind for the ordinary householder is the hang-on radiator humidifier, but there are many models available, suitable for all types of house. The Advisory Section staff of the Air Improvement Services will assist inquirers with unbiased and free advice.

Insulation and double glazing   These form part of the modernization programme and have already been touched on in previous chapters. Both amenities can quite well be incorporated into any old house and I have cited examples of where they have been done very successfully.

Bathrooms   Some old houses have never possessed a bathroom; others may have a very small one with out-of-date plumbing that badly needs replacing. Either way, the problem will usually be a matter of how to make the best use of space. In the case of the non-bathroom it will depend upon the room that can conveniently be spared from the rest of the house, always bearing in mind the position of the plumbing. Sometimes there is an overlarge bedroom that can be partitioned off to give the necessary space, or there may be a corner of a landing to spare. The householder should be able to assess the amount of room he wants and make some careful measurements beforehand.

One may have ideas about the kind of bathroom one wants, but basically the layout must be designed by an expert to ensure that fittings and pipework meet the regulations and by-laws of the local council and water authority. A reputable plumber should be able to advise in this respect. Good ventilation, efficient lighting and heating are essential, and there should also be adequate space for towel rails and storage. It is practical to tile the bath and shower area and there are a variety of ceramic tiles available, their price depending upon design and colour. Floor covering can be in almost any moisture resisting material, but, next to carpet, cork tiles are warmest underfoot. They are not difficult to lay on an even floor, but the tiles should be sealed after laying, although it is possible to buy them presealed. There are a number of large builders' merchants up and down the country where full bathroom layouts can be seen, or advice may be sought from the British Bathroom Council.

By a little judicious planning it is often possible to add an extra bathroom by making two large rooms into three. This was accomplished very successfully in a large Georgian house in Berkshire where the rather spacious eighteenth-century-style rooms are both pleasant and practical to live in. Nevertheless, a bathroom for guests was badly needed, so the bedroom that was set aside for their use was divided with a partition wall to make the much-needed bathroom. Next to this was the existing bathroom (very convenient for plumbing) but this was also overlarge, so another partition was put up between the two bathrooms to make a fine walk-in airing cupboard, which now also houses the washing machine, spin dryer and ironing board. This laundry equipment makes use of the same heater that serves the baths and basins, which is very advantageous. It was a piece of planning which made the best possible use of the large areas of floor space which could well be spared without detriment to the rest of the house.

Airing cupboards seem to be missing in many old houses but, given the space, the problem of making one is not insurmountable. Most older houses have plenty of cupboards but they have seldom been planned in order to utilize them to their full advantage. They can often be tailored to house stores and equipment in a way that gives quick and easy access to the contents.

Kitchens   A kitchen in an old house needs very careful planning to bring it right up to date, and it is better to take one's time over it rather than rush into a scheme that may turn out to be the opposite of labour-saving. If the room is well designed it should save both time and energy.

The basic art of kitchen planning is to have everything easily to hand. The ideal is to have a simple, rectangular room with adequate windows and the minimum number of doors arranged to give as much continuous wall space as possible, so that the necessary appliances can be installed in the correct relationship. This does not always work out in practice, for the housewife may find herself confronted with a long narrow room, or an awkwardly shaped one, neither of which was built to take modern equipment.

If you intend buying new units the kitchen-furniture specialist will offer worthwhile help in this area, but if you intend fitting your own make sure they are the right size to take any existing equipment and remember to seal between the units. There are also some very good floor and wall cabinets and easily fixed shelves available from shops dealing with do-it-yourself fittings. Either way, the aim should be to utilize as much space as possible in a small kitchen. The layout should not only be practical, it should be safe. Bearing in mind that some 40 per cent of accidents in the home happen in the kitchen, potentially dangerous situations should be avoided, as, for instance, placing a cooker or a hob underneath a window, where draughts could interfere with the cooking or blow gas jets out or, at worst, set fire to the curtains. If curtains are used, they should be anchored down firmly with rods top and bottom, or a better choice may be a blind.

Another source of danger is placing the cooker on the opposite side of the room to the sink. This creates a 'traffic route' which could cause accidents. The best layout is sink, drainer, work top, cooker, with the opposite wall left free for storage units and equipment. Obviously, the existing plumbing arrangements will have to be taken into account, and the shorter the run of pipes, the better.

Other small points of kitchen arrangements to be considered are good lighting, particularly over the sink – something which is often neglected in old houses; tiling behind the cooker or sink; altering a hinge to make a door open the other way, in some circumstances perhaps removing the door altogether, or installing sliding doors where space is limited.

Work surfaces need to be chosen carefully. Laminates are the least expensive and come in an attractive range of colours and patterns. They are reasonably heat resistant but they can scratch. If a marble slab can be incorporated somewhere it will be more than a luxury; it will be a lasting boon. Ceramic tiles need to be on a firm base, set in a waterproof grout, but they will be heat resistant except for pans of hot oil. Wood is also reasonably heat resistant and can be sealed, but otherwise needs oiling from time to time.

The floor of a kitchen should be water and grease resistant, non-slip and easy to clean. These are the first essential requirements but the material is open to choice, ranging from ceramic tiles, vinyl tiles and sheet flooring, to cork tiles, the latter with a hard-wearing seal.

The possibilities are stimulating to anyone with an inventive mind, for the kitchen is one of the areas in an old house that may be adapted to be as modern as you please without spoiling the character of the rest of the house. No doubt each housewife will have her own ideas which she wants to put into practice, and since she is the one who will spend a considerable part of her day in it, she should see to it that her wishes are carried out. Some of the best and most well-planned kitchens I have seen in period houses have been designed by the women who are to use them.

The whole house   In its broadest sense modernization covers the whole house. I refer particularly to houses that were built in Edwardian days, just before the turn of the century. They were built to last, of rosy red brick with some good detailed stonework, with gables, bay windows and even a small turret. There is nothing wrong with them to warrant wholesale restoration, but in many cases they do need to be brought up to date.

As an example, I saw one house of this period in a quiet, tree-lined avenue in Chiswick, London. 'An ordinary house, in an ordinary road, just like hundreds of others,' was how its owner, an architect by profession, described it.

True, the outside is undistinguished, one of a long row of semi-detached houses built at the time when London's suburbs were sprawling. It looks neat and trim with a small paved courtyard leading to a porch and a painted front door, but once the door opens all conventional ideas are exploded. Inside is a modern décor with a simplicity of line and fineness of detail which bring it superbly up to date. In the hall the long narrow look common to this type of house has given way to one of elegant sleekness, and the area is simply furnished with a table of one long piece of yew, bolted to the wall like a shelf.

The large front room with the traditional bay window is used as an office-cum-studio and is strictly a working domain. In fact, the

48 *An Edwardian semi-detached house in Chiswick, London, outwardly as it was when built at the beginning of the century*

49 Left: *The extension built on to the lounge at Chiswick, all completely modernized. To the left of the picture is a panel of mirror glass which is so much a feature of this house*

architect replanned this old house for himself because of its convenience and because his wife likes the protective feeling of an old building.

Houses of this period are apt to have dark corners and alcoves that do nothing for a room except destroy its symmetry, but in this case these awkward spots are deliberately used to make a feature. For instance, the space under the stairs has been made into a hanging cupboard for coats, with pull-out rails and coat hangers and a curtain in front. A door would not have been practical here.

The lounge, at the back of the house, originally had an open fireplace and french doors that led into the garden. Now, that exterior wall has been taken down and an extension built of the same kind of bricks as the rest of the house. Since it is built out to the full width of the house, there is almost three times the amount of floor space there was previously. To add to the feeling of spaciousness and light, wherever there are protuberances they are broken up by the use of mirrors, mere slots sometimes but they are none the less effective. The interior walls of the extension are faced with Canadian birch, but the wall to the garden is a vast expanse of glass – huge sliding doors to the patio which enable the colourful garden to be seen in all its beauty at all seasons. These doors are double glazed with sealed units which keep out noise as well as the cold, since this is a district where the constant loud drone of aircraft can be very disturbing. Double glazing and an insulated ceiling reduce it to a minimum.

When this extension was built a concrete floor was put in and underfloor gas warm-air heating was installed, which is also air conditioned and controlled to suit requirements, for this architect believes that radiators destroy a room layout. In every respect this is a strikingly modern room with its own unique character, a true reflection of the owners' tastes.

At the side of the house an old-fashioned breakfast room, which once contained a dresser and a large boiler with a high mantelpiece, has been converted into a fine modern dining room, conveniently placed with a door to the kitchen and another to the hall. An unwanted chimney breast is concealed without waste of space by being panelled over with Canadian cedar, the side recesses and space at the back being used for cupboards. These include a capacious sewing cupboard neatly tucked away behind double doors. There is a place for everything here and nothing obtrudes to detract from the dignity of natural wood.

The kitchen has been entirely redesigned. A scullery leading off it had its door removed and it is now converted into an open store cupboard, with narrow shelves, so that goods are both easy to see and to reach. The partition wall was shifted back 2 or 3 feet to make way for kitchen units, all of which have a cheerful red theme. At the opposite end a big larder was taken down to give room for the cooker, and an extra window with an extractor fan was put in, an alteration which made the kitchen spacious and light. The ceiling is well insulated with expanded polystyrene tiles which are cheap and warm and have no condensation problems. Heavy vinyl covers the walls and the floor is of Italian glazed ceramic tiles. Even the net curtains were designed to fit within the thickness of the frame of the original window and secured by rods top and bottom. No detail is lacking in this kitchen which is an object lesson in how space can be used to the utmost.

Upstairs, there were many awkward corners to conceal. In the principal bedroom two superb walls of pear wood, soft and satiny to the touch, disguise the chimney breast on one side and some odd angles on the other, the space between the panelling and the walls being made into cupboards with hanging space for clothes. In one corner an alcove is curtained off to take a wash basin and toilet accessories, lined with mirror glass to reflect light. It also forms an entry to both cupboards, so that they are completely concealed. The dressing table is one long formica shelf with a triple mirror over it which opens at each side to reveal shallow built-in shelves for cosmetics.

This is a house full of original ideas to set other owners of similar old homes thinking. The modernization has been done gradually, when a busy architect had time to spare for his own affairs, but that way there was time to choose carefully and the results have been supremely satisfying.

Interior decorations   From the very earliest times there has been some attempt to beautify the house by what we now call 'interior decoration', and these days this term covers everything to do with painting, papering, furniture and furnishings. In feudal manor houses wall hangings of tapestry or arras, with pictures of great events illustrated in fine needlework, served their purpose in keeping out draughts, but they also had great artistic merit and, now, historic value. A painted cloth was the more modest version of the costly tapestry hanging, but both of these were probably the forerunner of wallpapers. Many people do not realize that wallpaper is not a modern innovation. The earliest made in England dated from about 1509. It was based on the formalized damask pattern, the idea being that those who could not afford velvet or damask or leather on their walls could at least imitate them. Fine wallpapers have continued to be made in England ever since and all through the ages there have been attempts to copy the appearance of expensive textiles which prove that the old idea of wall hangings remains in favour.

Sometimes the act of scraping back to an original surface in an old house reveals some relics of former wallpapers of a design and quality that is never seen today. They were hand-blocked, made by craftsmen, whose colour sense was faultless. Any period room would look the richer and more beautiful for the addition of one of these wallpapers, and if one can afford it, it is possible to take a piece of an original wallpaper to a specialist manufacturer and get a block made, so that a room can be restored to its former character. This, of course, would mean getting an exclusive paper, and some may feel that this idea in itself would be worth the outlay. Failing that, a visit to one of the well-known manufacturers' showrooms will help decide on the kind of wallpaper that is suitable for a period house and there are always specially trained members of the staff to help and advise. In some places, period rooms, fully decorated and furnished, are set out for the customer to see. This is also a great help in choosing fabrics.

Books on furnishings of the period and visits to museums such as the Victoria & Albert, London, will be of considerable help to those planning their own decoration, but there are still some who prefer to consult the experts. Many firms of interior decorators run a specialist service of this kind and will gladly give advice, either by post or by personal call.

13
The Law

Many people chafe at the restrictions placed upon them by building regulations and planning laws, and in some respects they do seem to be weighted against the owners of period houses. For all that, they are by no means a modern innovation, for they go back to early medieval days when the close-packed houses of London were constantly menaced by fire and some form of protection was called for. Over the years a code of by-laws was drawn up whereby certain rules had to be obeyed or the offending building was pulled down. This still applies, in certain extreme cases, but on the whole the building regulations are designed for our protection and they ensure that we do at least live in more sanitary, healthy conditions than did our medieval forebears.

As with other forms of building, restoration is subject to regulations and the intending restorer should make himself familiar with them. He may need some preliminary advice in respect of his own particular type of house and this is available from the Society for the Protection of Ancient Buildings. As long ago as 1877 the public conscience was aroused by the wanton destruction of many of England's beautiful houses, with the result that William Morris, Philip Webb, John Ruskin and Sir Edward Burne-Jones founded this society, whose function is to advise owners and builders of the best methods to use in the preservation and restoration of old buildings. Their help is invaluable.

The law on historic buildings   If a building is scheduled as an ancient monument it is automatically protected by law and the owner or anyone else entitled to do work on it is legally bound to give three months' notice of such work or alteration to the Ministry of Public Building and Works, which primarily bears responsibility for all such buildings. If the work is carried out without permission the owner is liable to prosecution. Many old manor houses come under this ministerial protection and as a result they are admirably preserved as far as possible in their original state, with necessary modernization in keeping with the style of the building.

Many more houses, protected by being 'listed' as of special architectural or historic interest, come under the jurisdiction of the Ministry of Housing and Local Government or the Welsh Office. They include some quite small cottages if they have any architectural significance or have been associated with well-known characters or events. Such listed buildings are protected from demolition and from alterations that would spoil their character.

All buildings built before 1700 which survive in anything like their original condition are automatically listed. Thereafter, selection is necessary and a provisional graded list is issued to each local authority. On this basis a statutory list is compiled which makes all the buildings thereon legally subject to the provisions of the Town and Country Planning Act, 1968. The statutory lists may be inspected at the National Monuments Record, London, the Welsh Office, Cardiff, or at the office of the relevant county council, county borough or county district council. There is, therefore, every opportunity given for people to verify the status of their houses before carrying out any kind of work.

Under the old law it was necessary to give notice of the intention to alter or demolish a listed building and the local authority or the Minister then decided whether to make a 'Building Preservation Order'. Now, under the new Act, it is only necessary to get a 'listed building consent' from the local planning authority in a similar way to that for obtaining planning permission for building; but it is an offence to demolish or alter a listed building without this consent and the penalty can be a fine of unlimited amount, or up to twelve months' imprisonment, or both. If, however, alteration in the nature of development is proposed, specific planning permission is required which in this case will also count as listed building consent.

Before any demolition takes place, the application to do so must be advertised locally so that any amenity societies and members of the public have an opportunity to comment and have their remarks forwarded to the Minister.

A listed building is also protected from a careless owner; if he does not look after it the local authority may, with the Minister's consent, buy it compulsorily. If it is deliberately neglected in order to redevelop the site the local authority may be empowered to acquire the building at a price which excludes the value of the site for redevelopment. In this way historic buildings are protected on all sides. It is only when the hierarchy itself decrees their destruction in the name of progress that the cause is lost.

Even where a house is not listed, if the restoration required involves any structural alterations or improvements, it is still necessary to apply for planning permission from the local authority, giving full details of the work before it is begun. Some types of work can be done without such permission, but the wise house owner will find out exactly where he stands beforehand. The present building regulations apply throughout England and Wales with the exception of the inner London boroughs, which are controlled by the London Building Acts. Scotland has its own regulations, but they are similar. The old building by-laws, which they replaced, varied considerably from area to area. Whilst these regulations cannot be altered by local authorities, their interpretation of them can still vary from authority to authority; but they do at least allow for wide powers of relaxation by the authorities, and there is a right of appeal to the Minister against any local authority's refusal to relax, and his decision is usually uniform throughout the country.

The regulations have been amended a number of times since they were first introduced and the current statutory instrument is the Building Regulations Act, 1976, which is broken down into various different sections with a set of schedules relating to each one. It is a criminal offence to fail to meet the requirements of these regulations.

If you are going to carry out any form of structural alteration to your property you must deposit plans with the local authority according to the schedule that lays down the manner in which the drawings have to be produced, but your architect will know all about this and know exactly what is required.

Where an extension is involved planning permission does not necessarily mean that the building can go ahead without further hindrance. There are private rights to be considered, rights of way, neighbours' objections if light is blocked out, and other snags. However, with goodwill on both sides, these minor obstacles can usually be overcome, and it is, after all, in everyone's interest that buildings should conform to local standards.

Grants and loans Although listing does not give an owner an automatic right to a grant or loan for improving or maintaining a house, these are sometimes available both from central government funds and from local authorities. Government grants, as a rule, are limited to buildings of outstanding architectural or historical interest and the Minister is advised about their suitability by the Historic Buildings Council for England. Local authorities have greater scope and are not restricted to listed buildings, though they may give a 'house improvement grant' for improving or converting a listed building that is to be used as a dwelling. Concerned for old houses with a useful life ahead of them, the Housing Act of 1969 introduced more generous assistance for those who want to improve and modernize such homes.

There are now three types of grant available through local councils: for conversion; for the provision of standard amenities; and for the overall benefit of houses in multiple occupation. The first two are more likely to apply to the average owner of an old house, and providing he is the freeholder or holds a lease with at least five years unexpired, he is entitled to apply for a grant. He may have to produce a certificate from the Land Registry proving his ownership. Under these conditions he may then approach the local council, giving a brief outline of the proposed work, and he will be given an application form. Where the scheme is very ambitious (as in a full-scale conversion) he may have to submit plans, specifications and an estimate, in which case it is wise to seek professional advice. The premises will be inspected by a representative of the local authority before grant approval is given, and on no account should any work begin before this approval comes through or planning permission is given. These are two separate procedures.

The state of repair of a house is an important item to be considered when estimating the cost of any improvement scheme; even so, the grants are usually generous, but it must be emphasized that with the exception of the standard amenities grant, the local authorities have an absolute discretion over whether or not they give a grant. The policy laid down by the Department of the Environment may be interpreted differently from area to area, and conditions may vary. It is most important that the householder understands these conditions thoroughly before making a formal application for a grant. A visit to the local council is advisable.

Finally, the ambitious owner who has dreams of improving and enlarging his house should not forget that he is also increasing its rateable value at the same time, and if he is prudent he will inquire of his rating officer the amount by which his rates will increase should certain amenities be included.

Since the restoration of old buildings often requires the services of specialist craftsmen, a list of names and addresses of professional organizations and trade associations is appended at the end of this book, which will help inquirers. Where an architect is concerned, the Royal Institute of British Architects will require as much detailed information as possible on the house – type, size, location, use, historical importance and present condition – to allow them to choose a suitable person.

So, with all contingencies covered, it remains for the restorer to go ahead and inject new life into his own particular old house, creating his own private Shangri-La, and in so doing helping to preserve some of our rich heritage of old buildings for posterity.

Let me end by reiterating the arguments with which I began: that it is sound economy to recondition an old house; that such a house is more roomy and more adaptable than any comparable modern building; and that it is, above all, individualistic, with an atmosphere of its own that spells home, no matter whether it is a cottage or a castle.

Appendix: Professional Bodies and Trade Organizations

The professional bodies and trade organizations listed below will put inquirers in touch with local members for restoration work. Those suppliers referred to in the text are also listed.

Specialist architects
Royal Institute of British Architects,
66 Portland Place, London W1N 4AD

Specialist surveyors
Royal Institution of Chartered Surveyors,
12 Great George Street, London SW1

Incorporated Society of Valuers & Auctioneers,
3 Cadogan Gate, London, SW1

Specialist builders
Federation of Master Builders,
33 John Street, London WC1

Advice on building materials
Building Research Advisory Service,
Building Research Station, Garston, Watford WD2 7JR

Craftsmen
The Crafts Council, Conservation Section,
12 Waterloo Place, London SW1

For Scotland
The Conservation Officer, Conservation Bureau,
Scottish Development Agency, 102 Telford Road, Edinburgh EH4 2NP

Rural craftsmen (wrought-iron smiths, thatchers, pargeters, etc.)
Council for Small Industries in Rural Areas,
(Advisory Services Division), 141 Castle Street, Salisbury, Wiltshire, SP1 3TP

Roofing
National Federation of Roofing Contractors,
15 Soho Square, London W1

Hand-made roofing tiles
Swallow's Tiles (Cranleigh) Ltd,
Bookhurst Brick & Tile Works, Cranleigh, Nr Guildford, Surrey GU6 7DP

Slates
Penrhyn Quarries Ltd,
Bethesda, Nr Bangor, Gwynedd LL57 4YG, North Wales

Period building materials
The London Architectural Salvage and Supply Company,
Mark Street, London EC2A 4ER

Hand-moulded bricks
Bulmer Brick & Tile Company Ltd,
Bulmer, Nr Sudbury, Suffolk

Stained glass and leaded lights
Worshipful Company of Glaziers,
9 Montague Close, London SE1

Goddard & Gibbs Studios,
41–49 Kingsland Road, London EC2

Advice on timber
Timber Research and Development Association,
Hughenden Valley, High Wycombe, Buckinghamshire

British Wood Preserving Association,
150 Southampton Row, London WC1

Architectural woodcarving, cabinet making and joinery
Roger Board Ltd,
273 Putney Bridge Road, London SW15

Architectural ironmongery
Guild of Architectural Ironmongers,
15 Soho Square, London W1

J. D. Beardmore & Co. Ltd,
3 Percy Street, London W1

Victorian ironwork restorers
Wandle's Workshop,
200 Garratt Lane, London SW18 4ED

Garden statuary and stonework
Chilstone Garden Ornaments,
Sprivers Estate, Horsmonden, Kent TN12 8DR

Plasterwork
Worshipful Company of Plasterers,
1 London Wall, London EC2

G. Jackson & Sons Ltd,
Rathbone Works, Rainville Road, Hammersmith, London W6

Relief decoration and mouldings (polyurethane)
Copley Crafts,
Thorney Grange, Spennithorne, Leyburn, North Yorkshire DL8 5PW

Interior design
Interior Decorators and Designers Association,
24 Ormond Road, Richmond, Surrey TW10 6TH

British Bathroom Council,
Federation House, Station Road, Stoke-on-Trent ST4 2RT

Fireplaces
(For regional lists of approved advice centres)
The Solid Fuel Advisory Service,
Hobart House, Grosvenor Place, London SW1

The National Fireplace Council,
Churchill House, Hanley, Stoke-on-Trent

Ceramic tiles
H. & R. Johnson,
Highgate Tile Works, Tunstall, Stoke-on-Trent ST6 4JX

Electrical contractors
Electrical Contractors' Association,
32 Palace Court, London W2

Insulation
Department of Energy,
Thames House South, Millbank, London SW1P 4QT

Woodworm and dry rot
Rentokil Advice Centre,
Freepost, East Grinstead, West Sussex RH19 2BR

Air conditioning and humidity control
Air Improvement Services,
21 Napier Road, Bromley, Kent BR2 9JA

Heating and Ventilating Contractors' Association,
ESCA House, 34 Palace Court, London W2 4JG

Guidance on legislation
The Society for the Protection of Ancient Buildings,
55 Great Ormond Street, London WC1N 3JA

The Ministry of Housing and Local Government,
Whitehall, London SW1

National Monuments Record,
Fielden House, Great College Street, London SW1

Welsh Office,
Summit House, Windsor Place, Cardiff

Permanent exhibition of building materials and information centre
The Building Centre,
26 Store Street, Tottenham Court Road, London WC1

Bibliography

Geoffrey Beard, *Decorative Plasterwork in Great Britain*, Phaidon Press, 1975

Alec Clifton-Taylor, *The Pattern of English Building*, Faber & Faber, 1972

Banister F. Fletcher and H. Phillips Fletcher, *The English Home*, Methuen, 1910

W. H. Godfrey, *Our Building Inheritance*, Faber & Faber, 1944

Kenneth Hudson, *Building Materials*, Longman, 1972

Donald Insall, *The Care of Old Buildings Today*, Architectural Press, 1972

Architectural History, Journal of the Society of Architectural Historians of Great Britain, Vol. 24, 1981

Hugh Lander, *The Do's and Don't's of Cottage Conversion*, Acanthus Books, 1982

  House and Cottage Interiors, Acanthus Books, 1982

The Thatcher's Craft, Rural Industries Bureau, 1961

Alastair Service, *Edwardian Architecture*, Thames & Hudson, 1977

Pointing Stone and Brick Walling and *Cleaning Stone and Brick*, Technical Pamphlets 4 and 5, Society for the Protection of Ancient Buildings, 1977

Index

Page numbers in italic refer to illustrations